ENDORSEMENTS

Terry Nance's book, *God's Armorbearer*, is an insightful look at a neglected ministry that needs desperately to be rekindled in the kingdom. I believe it is essential for every sincere Christian to read and apply. That is the reason I purchased 5,000 of them for use at our church, The Potter's House. I would simply be afraid to command any troops into battle who had not read it.

Bishop T.D. Jakes

This book has been a familiar friend to me ever since I was a young man. My father, Don Nori Sr., had me read this book to prepare me to serve the authors we were publishing. It became my foundation for how to work with the most anointed men and women of God in the Church today. Throughout my career, I have traveled with them and carried their bags and served them. This character-building book raised me to be an armorbearer, and it will do the same for you!

Don Nori
CEO, Destiny Image/Nori Media Group

Over the years I have given literally thousands of Terry's first edition of *God's Armorbearer* to Teen Challenge leaders around the world. It has always been an amazing book to train upcoming leaders on what it means to be a servant and to know how to serve those you follow. I can say with extreme excitement that I feel Terry has once again captured the essence of what it means to be a servant leader with this generation. I would encourage you to not only read this book for yourself but to purchase one for every leader who serves with you. I am anxious to get this new edition in the hands of our Teen Challenge family globally.

Jerry Nance, Ph.D.
President, Global Teen Challenge

Pastor Terry Nance's first book, *God's Armorbearer,* was an inspiration and a go-to resource for my learning about servant leadership. I gave dozens of copies away to those I was training up to lead. For a time, this book was in almost every pastor's home I visited. The impact of Terry's revelation about armorbearers can without exaggeration sit on many leader's top-ten book list over the last 40 years. After living what he wrote about for many years now, Pastor Terry offers an update with fresh revelation. This book will no doubt touch new generations of leaders as they learn the ways of service and honor. And I hope it will encourage mature leaders to step up as mentors and coaches to bless coming generations. I highly recommend this book.

E. Wayne Drain
Founding pastor of City Church
(formerly Fellowship of Christians)
President of Wayne Drain Ministries
Author, songwriter, and leadership advisor

God knew that in the right season author and pastor Terry Nance would be ready to write this timely book. Terry is known globally for introducing the biblical role of armorbearers in his bestselling volumes of armorbearer books. Terry is the right man to share what God has given to him for armorbearers for the next generation.

This revelation is thirty years old and reaching into the next generation. This is time-tested and proven to be essential for endtime harvest. Terry humbly addresses the confusion that some misguided individuals have taken with the armorbearer teaching. This clear, anointed book promotes servanthood and honor and not selfishness and greed. This book will not only bless you but properly equip you to fulfill the honorable roll of an armorbearer.

Pastor Steve Dixon
Christian Life Cathedral
Fayetteville, Arizona
Chairman, Worldwide Evangelism

Since early 1991, I have grown up under Pastor Terry Nance's ministry. *God's Armorbearer* made an enormous impact on my life by imparting a love for Jesus, His leaders, and His Church. Terry's new book is now calling forth the leaders of the Body of Christ to be filled with the love of the "Father heart of God" and to reach this nation and the world's younger generations. It's time for the leaders to be spiritual fathers and mothers and the armorbearers to be spiritual sons and daughters. Our collective hearts should be broken for and turn toward these—our future leaders, our prodigal sons and daughters, and those in bondage to the spirit of the world! Chaos and dark demonic activity are determined to divide us from them, but we will run to them! Powerful, strategic, reformation, restoration!

Be blessed, moved, and transformed as you receive a great impartation of the love of our Father God through this book!

Philip Blunk
President of Arkansas Awakening
Associate Pastor, Impact Church Sherwood, Arkansas

Endorsements

from SPIRITUAL SONS *and* DAUGHTERS

God's Armorbearer for the Next Generation is a refreshing word inspired by the Spirit to release once again true unity in the Body of Christ. When embraced with an open heart, this book will ignite passion and restoration between leaders and servant-followers, dreamers and visionaries. I have had the privilege to learn and serve under Pastors Terry and Kim Nance for about three years, and they have truly set it upon themselves to both listen to and train me, as well as establish a culture for other elders and leaders to do the same. The result, for me personally, is a passion to carry the vision of what is truly my home church and a true love and armorbearer spirit for my leaders.

Michaela Cozad

This book is a fresh word for the Body of Christ and a very powerful and insightful guide to being an armorbearer for your pastors and leaders from an author who continues to serve as an armorbearer himself. Being around Pastor Terry Nance and his ministry has changed my life and has shown me how to be an armorbearer. He has personally invested his time to pour into my life, and it's more than an honor to serve as an armorbearer for someone like Pastor Terry Nance.

Jason Allen

My first time picking up Pastor Terry's book, *God's Armorbearer*, I was volunteering for a disaster relief mission group. Little did I know, at the time, God would ask me to serve Pastor Terry as well as his wife on staff at their church. The words on the pages of his book taught me to honor and serve my leadership to the best of my ability. What a privilege that God choose me to serve under the armorbearer.

Through the years, Pastor Terry and Mrs. Kim became my spiritual parents. As you read the words in this book, let them flow into your heart. Pastor Terry's words will truly change the dynamic in your church. This book is meant to bridge the gap between the generations, to allow this generation to be heard, and for the older generation to be honored.

Being Pastor and Mrs. Kim's armorbearer was great, but being a spiritual daughter was so much better! They value my opinion, they take the time to listen, and they allow me to be creative and flow with vision. Because they take their time to listen and build relationship with me, I want to honor them even more.

If you will allow the words in this book to be written on your heart, they will change not only how you serve but how you lead!

Erica Hale

I met Pastor Terry while waiting tables at Hideaway Pizza. I was at a very broken point in my life, with a broken heart and terrible church hurt. He and a few others were my very last table of the night. They had asked to pray with me, gave me a prophetic word, and invited me to their church. I was shocked to find out Pastor Terry was the author of *God's Armorbearer*. It was a book my previous pastor had me read years earlier and it changed my life! After reading it, I dedicated myself to bearing the armor of my leaders with honor and integrity. After leaving that church, the relationship that I had with the pastor had dwindled and I had felt like an orphan.

Pastor Terry and several other spiritual mothers and fathers took me in and helped me surrender the hurt and offense that I held in my heart for so long toward my previous church and church leaders.

Healing pierced my heart whenever Pastor Terry said this: "You're a daughter of mine. True fathers give their children the freedom to come and go as they please. You can leave and you will still be my daughter."

God's Armorbearer for the Next Generation brings healing to those like me who simply want the freedom to be the sons and daughters of the generation that came before us without fear of being disowned or forgotten.

Taylor Raborn

I have been sitting under the ministry of Pastor Terry Nance and his lovely wife, Kim, for about seven years. We can say without a doubt they are the real deal. My husband Eric and I first got a glimpse into the heart of my pastor through the first *God's Armorbearer* book—and then when he came to us saying he was going to write one for our generation, we were thrilled! We laughed and cried through reading this as the Holy Spirit used it to minister to us in ways we hadn't even known we needed! This book will bring healing to so many young people in ministry as it has brought healing to us. To God be the glory!

Eric and Jeannie Miller

God's Armorbearer for the Next Generation is an amazing book! It's a must read for the Body of Christ and I am confident that it will break barriers and challenge you as a follower of Jesus no matter what church you serve in. I encourage you to read this book as it gives insight on how to bear one another's burdens, bridging the gap between age groups and honoring one another in all things. I believe the goal is becoming so desperate to understand each other for the sake of the gospel that in the process we develop a passionate desire to carry it beyond the four walls of the church, as well as the generations to follow. I am sure this will be the outcome of a future armorbearer who takes the time to read this book and applies it to his/her life.

Pastors Terry and Kim Nance are such wonderful spiritual parents! They especially spend time in fellowship, listening to us and dreaming with us. Really, we are the same age at heart and that makes it so easy to be ourselves and who God has called us to be together. Even if we are still in the process of what God is doing in us, our spiritual parents are cheering us on, praying for us, and supporting us in any way they can. If we have a God dream, they want to hear it. And if we are dealing with unforeseen circumstances or even hardships, they thank the Lord for our provision, pray for us, help us, lend an ear and listen, and normally end the talk with a good laugh or two. Most importantly they are pouring truth and love into us, helping us in ministry, and believing with us for the next big things in our lives! What else could be better? I would choose to serve them over and over! I am so proud to be one of their spiritual daughters and I love them dearly.

Mandie Allen

GOD'S ARMOR BEARER

FOR THE NEXT GENERATION

GOD'S
ARMOR
BEARER

FOR THE NEXT GENERATION

TERRY NANCE

DESTINY IMAGE® PUBLISHERS, INC.

P.O. Box 310, Shippensburg, PA 17257-0310

"Promoting Inspired Lives."

This book and all other Destiny Image and Destiny Image Fiction books are available at Christian bookstores and distributors worldwide.

For more information on foreign distributors, call 717-532-3040.

Reach us on the Internet: www.destinyimage.com.

ISBN 13 TP: 978-0-7684-5432-1

ISBN 13 eBook: 978-0-7684-5433-8

ISBN 13 HC: 978-0-7684-5435-2

ISBN 13 LP: 978-0-7684-5434-5

For Worldwide Distribution, Printed in the U.S.A.

1 2 3 4 5 6 7 8 / 24 23 22 21 20

CONTENTS

INTRODUCTION

W hat is an armorbearer? That was the question I asked the Holy Spirit the night He spoke to my heart: "I want you to serve your pastor as an armorbearer."

The answer to my question was found in First Samuel.

And Jonathan said to his young armor-bearer, Come, and let us go over to the garrison of these uncircumcised; it may be that the Lord will work for us. For there is nothing to prevent the Lord from saving by many or by few. And his armor-bearer said to him, Do all that is in your mind; I am with you in whatever you think [best]. ...Then Jonathan climbed up on his hands and feet, his armor-bearer after him; and the enemy fell before Jonathan, and his armor-bearer killed them after him (1 Samuel 14:6-7,13 AMPC).

An armorbearer was one who prepared the weapons of his leader, listened to the heart of his leader, and fought alongside with complete trust in the direction of his leader's guidance. This message from the Lord sent me on a 23-year journey to follow my leader through the good, the challenging, and the heartbreaks of ministry. All this comes as we walk together through the seasons of ministry.

Now God is calling a new generation of armorbearers to stand with their leaders for a new fresh revival of His presence. If this is to happen, reformation needs to come. My desire is to release this armorbearer spirit into this now generation. What I have discovered is this new generation is crying out for relational leaders and not just positional leaders. I call this the Malachi Reformation.

> *Behold, I will send you Elijah the prophet before the coming of the great and dreadful day of the Lord. And he will turn the hearts of the fathers to the children, and the hearts of the children to their fathers, lest I come and strike the earth with a curse* (Malachi 4:5-6).

The apostle Paul said we have ten thousand instructors in Christ but few fathers. The Church is full of instructors, but not spiritual fathers.

So where are we now in this season? God is calling the pastors to become spiritual fathers and mothers and the armorbearers to be sons and daughters. With this new revelation from God for today in my heart, I brought together a group of Millennials to my home who are sons and daughters in the ministry. This first chapter is what they had to say.

I pray that revelation of this truth will connect with the hearts of spiritual leaders, causing the Body of Christ to become one.

— 1 —

WILL YOU PLEASE
FORGIVE ME?

Wow! Thirty years have passed since an unknown associate pastor wrote a book titled *God's Armorbearer* that introduced a revelation that would go around the world. To this day we don't know how many people it has reached. But now, here is my dilemma. The Holy Spirit is prompting me to reintroduce this revelation to a new generation that very possibly has been hurt and abused by leadership. Maybe this is you, and because of this hurt you may have lost trust in your parents, teachers, marketplace managers, pastors and/or spiritual leaders.

How can I get you to keep reading and hear from my heart what the Holy Spirit is saying to you personally through me? *God is not condemning you for what you are not; He is here and always ready to reveal who you are to Him.*

This dilemma has driven me to make a new, fresh appointment with God every morning to seek and receive His wisdom. As the apostle John says in Revelation 1:10: *"I was in the Spirit on the*

Lord's day." I am also by His grace waiting on God for fresh manna to inspire, instruct, and bring love to all who carry an offense against leadership, guiding you back to your divine destiny for this planet. If you don't quite know what I mean, God wants you to understand exactly why you are who you are. Understanding your divine destiny answers your big *why!* You have to know your WHY to find your YES!

While calling on the Lord for wisdom, He prompted me to invite five Millennials to my home before I began this manuscript to ask their perspective on this new book. Here is what they said to me, "Pastor, you must ask us to forgive you and your generation for speaking down to us, offending us, and attempting to require us to read a book like the *Armorbearer."*

I have to say my heart was moved with compassion as they shared their stories. Why haven't I as their pastor taken the time to listen to them? Have I been too busy preaching vision over relationship? Four of the five of these young adults had been hurt by Christian leaders.

To the pastors and leaders who may be reading this, hang on just a minute. We are sharing with young people about being armorbearers, being the Aarons and Hurs to those God has brought to assist us, to hold up our hands as we minister to a hurting world. But before I go any further, I have to, by the Holy Spirit, lead this generation through a prayer that will begin healing and hopefully renew their love for ministry and the local church.

To all the Millennials, Generation Zs, and all others who have been hurt, wounded, and abused, I stand for myself and all pastors, ministers, and marketplace managers—please in the name of

Jesus forgive us! We are visionaries and at times we get ahead of our people. We love you and want nothing but restoration.

At a conference recently, I saw a beautiful couple who had been on my team a few years ago. Strange things happened during a time of transition with me and the church, and these two were hurt and then left. I knew I hurt them, but my pride said they weren't armorbearers, so just let them go. We spiritual leaders are called to be visionaries and sometimes we miss it. I missed it big time. During a meeting we were attending, the Holy Spirit quickened me to go and ask forgiveness from them. The husband wasn't there, but I took the opportunity to tell the wife how much Kim and I loved them and would she please forgive me for not being the model of Jesus to them that I should have been.

In her incredible response, she asked me to please forgive her for missing it also. God's love set us both completely free. When spiritual leaders ask forgiveness and the person says in return, "Please forgive me," something supernatural takes place. The glory of Jesus falls from Heaven and healing begins. Forgiveness is always freeing to the one forgiving. I didn't completely understand the power of forgiveness until these wonderful Millennials instructed me concerning the most powerful words on this planet, "Please forgive me!" It is like the divine Trinity—unity is restored.

> *Behold, how good and how pleasant it is for brethren to dwell together in unity! It is like the precious oil upon the head, running down on the beard, the beard of Aaron, running down on the edge of his garments. It is like the dew of Hermon, descending upon the mountains of*

Zion; for there the Lord commanded the blessing—life forevermore (Psalm 133:1-3).

It takes us all working together to build a unified Church.

Pastors, leaders, parents, and marketplace managers, it is time we ask for forgiveness. We must humble ourselves to ask forgiveness if we want unity to flow in our midst. Now all you beautiful young students and young adults, it's time to forgive. Forgive us all!

When we forgive, wonderful things happen. Forgiveness:

- Releases the oil of Heaven
- Allows humility to be the master of your emotions
- Breaks the devil's hold on your soul
- Releases the balm of Gilead to soothe the wound in your heart (Jeremiah 8:22)
- Defines the love of Jesus for all to see
- Restores the joy of your salvation
- Brings angels on the scene
- Is the ministry of reconciliation
- Breaks you free from the tormentors
- Puts you on the level of Heaven as you forgive like Jesus
- Reveals the armorbearer spirit—servanthood

The devil is not afraid of a big church, he's afraid of a unified Church!

Forgiveness is a stream of God that runs through our souls to the hurts and wounds of another. It bathes us in His glorious grace and we get to taste the Tree of Life from Heaven. It soothes all trouble and drama in our lives and introduces us to real peace.

After visiting for a time with these young adults, I felt like Jonathan and David as it says their souls were joined together. Two beautiful things happened that night. First, they asked if they could anoint me with oil and pray over the writing of this book. They not only prayed for me but began to speak by the Holy Spirit prophetic words that restored an apostolic anointing on my life.

Second, my youth pastor looked at me and said, "I am representing my generation and I am asking you to forgive us for not honoring you and your generation." I said, "I ask you to forgive me and my generation for not sitting down to listen to you." Do you get the picture here? My generation demands to be honored while the younger generation demands to be heard. That is the catch-22, the "Great Dilemma"—who gives in first?

Sometimes we elders say, "I'm not going to listen to someone who doesn't honor me," while our young pioneers say, "We will not honor you if you will not take the time to listen and lead through relationship and not by position."

Malachi gave us the answer years ago, prophesying to us all about this dilemma. God holds us responsible for this word:

Behold, I will send you Elijah the prophet before the coming of the great and dreadful day of the Lord. And he will turn the hearts of the fathers to the children, and the hearts of the children to their fathers, lest I come and strike the earth with a curse (Malachi 4:5-6).

Do we get what God is saying to us? If we don't yield to the voice of this word, we will bring a curse on our generation. Can we in the Body of Christ not recognize the demonic curse that is trying to come on the youth of this planet? God is not bringing it on us, we are releasing it through our own disobedience. Satan is trying to kill off a move of God in the earth. And He is using us and our prideful hearts as the tools.

So who gives in first? *"I will turn the hearts of the fathers to the children."* According to this Scripture, I do! I give in first. I humbly ask my children and my spiritual children to forgive me. Will others of my generation join me? A real father desires to sit and listen to the sons and daughters; and then the children will, with honor, wait for the wisdom and instruction of the father. They release honor and trust through relationship.

I am sharing a real revelation into the true calling of every leader. We are called to father, not just lead. This generation is crying for relationship and we must take up the mantle of Elijah and turn our hearts toward our sons and daughters. Not only our natural sons and daughters, but also our spiritual sons and daughters. Unity always happens in the Spirit, not by blood. The Lord said through Malachi that it would happen—and it is happening now. Intentional relational discipleship is what our Master Jesus modeled for us. His armorbearers, His apostles, died for their spiritual Father, Jesus, based on intentional relational discipleship.

I share more about this important aspect of relationship later on in its own chapter.

Now I speak to the readers who are 18 years old all the way to the 50-year-olds. It is time to move forward into your calling and destiny. You have a godly inheritance, but satan has stolen your calling through some kind of offense. You battle with trusting leaders and have laid down your gift because of the hurt. Listen to me! God needs you to respond to this question: What would Love do?

> *Therefore **be imitators of God** as dear children. And **walk in love**, as Christ also has loved us and given Himself for us, an offering and a sacrifice to God for a sweet-smelling aroma* (Ephesians 5:1-2).

So tell me, what do you smell like? What does your attitude smell like? *We are to produce the aroma of Heaven and not the stink of our culture.* What would Love do? This question and God's answer is for all believers to walk and live by. This is not a suggestion but a command from the Spirit of God. To live free, we have to forgive and move on!

Okay—are you ready? It's time to act like Jesus, our true Master and Savior. Let's forgive! Will you please forgive me? As I represent not only myself but the leaders who have hurt you, I ask God to forgive us for not walking in the mindset of Christ and hurting or misusing you in any way. I love you and ask you to release me, and all spiritual leaders, parents, pastors, and marketplace managers.

I pray for the spirit of joy to begin flowing into your heart. I love you and I am for you.

Now it's your turn. Take the leader in your heart, whoever he or she is, and pray:

> *"First of all God, please forgive me for my unforgiveness. This is sin against You and You only. I call on the blood of Jesus to heal my heart and emotions now. Father, forgive me for holding an offense against my leaders. To my leaders, I ask you to forgive me. I have held you in a place that I shouldn't have, but I choose to let this animosity go now. I love you and I bless you and your family with the love of Heaven. I am sure I may have hurt you in some way or disappointed you, but I ask for your forgiveness, in Jesus' name!"*

Wow! I feel the Spirit of God was just released into you and something is broken off your heart. Healing come now to this reader. I sense God is restoring you in a powerful way. Receive it in Jesus' name.

You may ask, "Brother Terry, what should I do now?" If the Lord compels you to go make it right with your leader face to face, then do it. But if you don't get the response you would like, don't get offended again. You have done your part. You are released! It is up to God to bring reconciliation. Sometimes we are looking for something that will never happen. It may not be reconciled, but it has been forgiven on your part. If you need a hug and you can't get one from that person, come find me and I will give you one for them. Of course that may not be physically possible because of locale, but I want you to know I love you. I want you to know how proud God is of you because you decided to move on. Now your calling is back on track!

Now let's move on to Chapter 2. I am about to pour my life into this book and share the awesome calling of the armorbearer. *Jesus is the ultimate Armorbearer.* He came down from His Father, laid down His own will, picked up His Father's dream, and thus God fulfilled every dream in His heart. He has been exalted King of kings and Lord of lords over Heaven, earth, and hell. We are called to model Jesus! Jesus taught us how to father, pastor, and be an armorbearer. He raised up armorbearers around Him who served Him in His ministry. These men carried His dream forward and shook the world for Him. These servant-leader armorbearers became His apostles.

As I begin this book, I share the statement the Lord gave me thirty years ago when I finished the manuscript. I stopped, took a breath, and asked Jesus to give me something to close that book with and He said, *"The armorbearers of today will be the leaders of tomorrow!"*

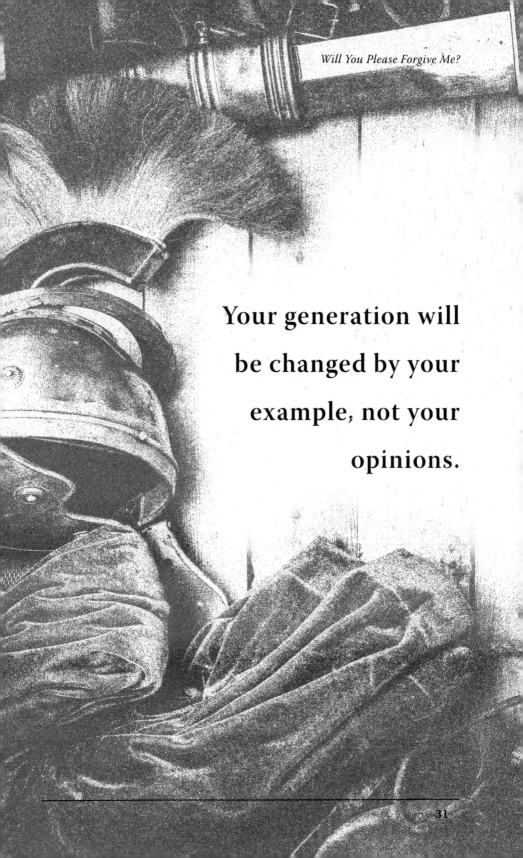

Your generation will be changed by your example, not your opinions.

— 2 —

WHAT IS AN ARMORBEARER?

Hallelujah! Healing and restoration is here now for the Church. The Holy Spirit is ready to impart the spirit of an armorbearer back into your life. Now we have to get into the truth of what the Holy Spirit is leading us into. We have to deal with some challenging issues, but now we have hearts to hear and ears to listen and obey. Let's look at ourselves and be willing to ask some difficult questions.

The Lord said He would not despise a broken and a contrite heart (Psalm 51:17). Through my own brokenness and love for the local church, I can truly pray that we all become armorbearers together, true warriors for Jesus.

How many books have been written about servant leadership or Jesus the Servant Leader? Needless to say, tons. Now, how many books have been written about Jesus as the Servant Follower? I have never run across any. Here is a truth—you have to build servanthood into your Christian foundation. You will never rise to the level of a leader until you first learn to follow.

The Bible says this about our Master Jesus: *"So Jesus explained, 'I tell you the truth, the Son can do nothing by himself. He does only what he sees the Father doing. Whatever the Father does, the Son also does'"* (John 5:19 NLT). Jesus, the Son of God was totally submitted to His Father. He never did anything unless He cleared it with His Father.

Now, how do we measure up to that? Have we submitted our lives and ministry to the spiritual men and women (God's elders) He has placed around us to speak into our lives? Hang on! I know the word *submitted* is not a politically correct word to use anymore. So let's use the word *yielded* to help us all adapt, even though God says submit. The word "submit" means to yield your soul and emotions. Again let's remember we are to model Jesus.

I'm going to share my personal struggles in this area later, but I want to proceed with this in mind: *the Bible is the infallible Word of God and is the absolute final authority in every decision I make.* That truth has to be foundational in our lives. If we don't believe that, then we are left to making choices based on our fallible opinions, which will not bring us into Kingdom living where Jesus is Lord.

If Jesus walked into your church right now and desired to be a member, He would go to the pastor and ask what He could do to serve and be a blessing to that church. Think about that statement for a moment. The responsibility rests on us as church members. Let's remember Ephesians 5:1 (NLT), *"Imitate God, therefore, in everything you do, because you are his dear children."* That is a two-way street. But what we are dealing with here is being a true servant-follower.

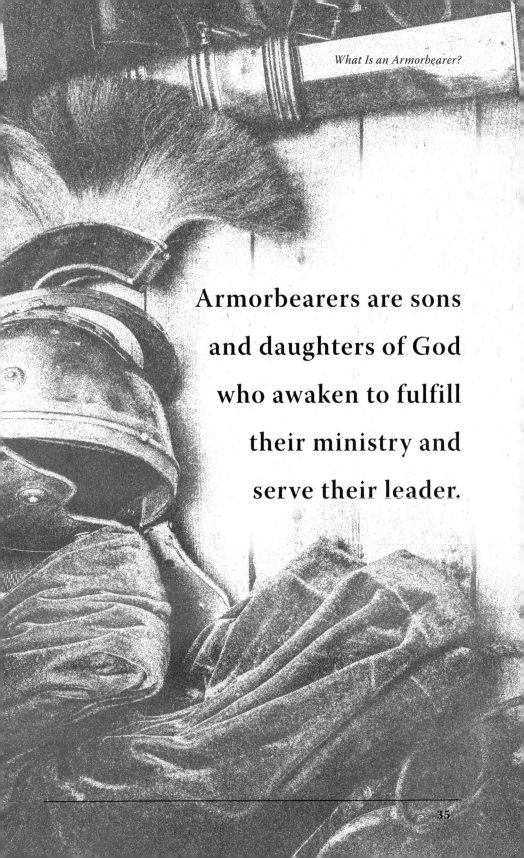

Armorbearers are sons
and daughters of God
who awaken to fulfill
their ministry and
serve their leader.

Our present culture is a demonic, rebellious antichrist culture. Facebook, Twitter, Instagram, and other social media sites promote violence and rebellion against authority. My children were taught by the public school system to question all authority. Thank God they knew better than to believe that falsehood, because Jesus is the head of our home. But let's be honest, pastors and leaders right now are almost dying under the load of carrying the responsibility of the church.

Across the board in the United States, local church attendance as well as finances are down. The accepted theology in today's culture is that the church is unnecessary and declares, "I'm not about to submit to or trust someone or give anyone the opportunity to take something from me." This ideology is a demonic assignment that Jesus will break through with the renewal of revival and the armorbearer spirit. The truth is, you must do both—submit and trust—to move, grow, and win in this present age.

Jesus set the example for us—and His Spirit is calling us back to holding up the arms of our leaders, even if we get a smell of BO! The love of Jesus and the Spirit of servanthood, the armorbearer, is being released now into the Body of Christ. True spiritual joy was released in me as I felt a group of Millennials embrace me and take my arms and hold them up in prayer. Even now they are choosing to surround my life as armorbearers, fasting and praying for me as I write this manuscript. I'm not just their leader, I have become a spiritual father in their faith.

My prayer is that the Holy Spirit will melt our hearts as we read through these pages and learn how to serve and bless one another as Jesus did. Always ask yourself this question, "What would Love do?"

"Brother Terry, you said that in the last chapter." Well it bears repeating. What would Love do? That's our standard. We have no option. We are mandated to live that way—as Jesus lived.

Armorbearer Revelation

Let me digress here, and tell you how the revelation concerning the armorbearer came to me. I was in my third year serving as an associate pastor. One evening in 1983, at the age of 26 years old, I felt a prompting to get alone with the Lord. My wife, Kim, and I had been reminiscing about all the things God had done in our lives to that point. We had just concluded the first graduation of our Mission School, and seven families were about to head across the ocean on the adventure of their lives for Jesus. They were moving to other countries to preach the Kingdom of God and to establish ministries.

We were so excited and so young, and we knew God was fulfilling a dream in our hearts. I had recently returned home from a trip through Asia where I had been for three weeks with Lester Sumrall and thirty other leaders. I was truly thankful to be included and privileged to travel with him. In the 1950s, Brother Sumrall had cast the devil out of a girl in the Philippines who was actually being bitten by devils. Through this incredible deliverance, a revival was ushered into the nation. Hundreds of thousands had been saved. The story will make your jaw drop at the awesome power of God flowing through this man.

Kim and I were working in a great church and running with a vision God had placed in my heart for the world. God was definitely fulfilling this vision, allowing me to be in the company of some of God's greatest men and women of faith. We took a moment that night and began to praise God for the beautiful favor He had placed on our lives. Suddenly I heard in my heart, "Pull away now to seek Me!" So, I went into our living room and began to pray. Then I was quickened in my spirit to read the story of David and Saul. I knew the Lord was ready to reveal something to me.

As I began to read, I came to First Samuel 16:21: *"So David came to Saul and stood before him. And he loved him greatly, and he became his armorbearer."* Suddenly the Lord quickened the word "armorbearer" to me. He said, "I have called you to be your pastor's armorbearer." At first I thought I was just hearing things, but I knew I was under a very heavy presence of God and I was receiving a mandate for my life. I quickly said out loud, "What in the world is an armorbearer?"

I knew I just read something about Jonathan and his armorbearer, so I went back to the story in First Samuel:

> *Then Jonathan said to the young man who bore his armor, "Come, let us go over to the garrison of these uncircumcised; it may be that the Lord will work for us. For nothing restrains the Lord from saving by many or by few." So his armorbearer said to him, "Do all that is*

in your heart. Go then; here I am with you, according to your heart" (1 Samuel 14:6-7).

I thought my heart was about to explode as I read that. Then again the voice of the Lord came to me, "You will lay down your vision and take up the vision of your pastor. You will support and serve him to the best of your ability. You are to take the vision of the house as your own."

Now you may think that I should have rejoiced in an incredible way and said, "Thank You, Jesus, for that glorious assignment!" But I didn't. I fell to the floor and began to cry out, "What about *my* vision? What about the vision I had in a field at 21 years old when You showed me the nations of the world? Just exactly what are You going to do with that?"

He then spoke peace and grace into me and said, "Terry, if you will run with the vision of your pastor, I will take you places you never dreamed you could go. I am not asking you to do something that I didn't do Myself. I laid down My desires and fulfilled my Father's dream and can you see what My Father did for Me?"

I wept like a baby for over an hour. I repented, yielded, and responded to the call. Some would say, "That's great, but that was for you." I would say let's allow Jesus to declare who it is for.

Let nothing be done through selfish ambition or conceit, but in lowliness of mind let each esteem others better than himself. Let each of you look out not only for his own interests, but also for the interests of others (Philippians 2:3-4).

Who, being in the form of God, did not consider it robbery to be equal with God, but made Himself of no reputation, taking the form of a bondservant, and coming in the likeness of men. And being found in appearance as a man, He humbled Himself and became obedient to the point of death, even the death of the cross. Therefore God also has highly exalted Him and given Him the name which is above every name (Philippians 2:6-9).

We are called to be armorbearers and carry someone else's shield. But let's start with carrying the vision of your local church. I had a phone call one day and the person accused me of trying to take an Old Testament office and bring it into the New. I explained that the armorbearer is not an office, but the same attitude Jesus modeled in Philippians 2. We are all called to be armorbearers in the likeness of Jesus.

What does an armorbearer do? In Old Testament days, he was responsible for carrying his master's shield into battle. He had the awesome responsibility of seeing to the safety of his officer. God was sure getting my priorities in order at that time in my life. It is my prayer that as you read this book, He will do the same for you. We have to change in order for God to breathe new life and usher in a real revival in the Church.

We live in a world that seems to know very little about laying down one's life for another. A full understanding of this concept is vital for Christians, especially if we know we have been called into the ministry.

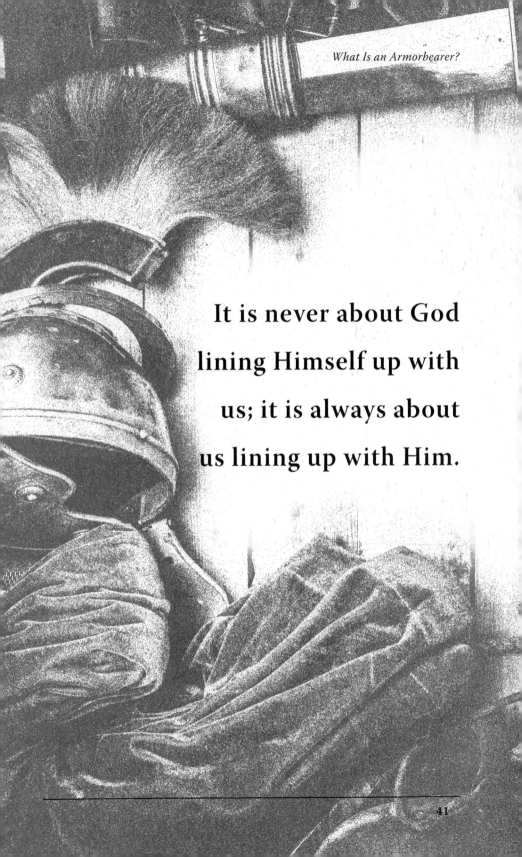

It is never about God lining Himself up with us; it is always about us lining up with Him.

Recently my 20-year-old daughter, McKenna, came home and said, "Dad, we have to talk." She's an intern at Youth America and Church of the Harvest in Oklahoma City. She said, "It's a Dad and daughter talk on the back porch."

Well, I knew this was serious. We headed to the porch and she began to pour her heart out to me about ministry. She said, "Dad, God has called me to the ministry."

Wow! The very thing I had refused to encourage to happen in her growing years, has come to her. I was not going to put my call on her because I knew God is the only One who can call someone to ministry. I made a decision that my kids would always come before my ministry.

I told McKenna that day on the porch how proud I was of her. I told her I knew she had been a real armorbearer to the ministry in Oklahoma City, and was glad she represented Jesus and her parents so well. She didn't mind carrying their shield and protecting her leaders. They knew she was committed and a tither to their church. She had also won several leadership awards. We were so proud of the Christian woman she had become.

Today, instead of offering ourselves to serve others, we in the church often expect others to wait on us. This is particularly true of our attitude toward the man or woman of God in our lives.

We will never flow in the anointing of Elisha until we have learned to serve an Elijah. Look carefully at the calling of Elisha to Elijah as his servant: *"Also you shall anoint Jehu the son of Nimshi as king over Israel. And **Elisha** the son of Shaphat of Abel Meholah you shall anoint as **prophet** in your place"* (1 Kings 19:16).

Elijah was to anoint Elisha as prophet in his place. Wow! Elisha is about to be introduced to the prophetic ministry of Elijah, who was one of the greatest prophets who ever lived. I bet when he anoints him, Elisha will start prophesying all over the place. He will bring the glory into the services before Elijah even gets up to preach. Elisha will increase while Elijah decreases. So here we go with the transfer of the anointing:

> *So he departed from there, and found Elisha the son of Shaphat, who was plowing with twelve yoke of oxen before him, and he was with the twelfth. Then Elijah passed by him and threw his mantle on him. And he left the oxen and ran after Elijah, and said, "Please let me kiss my father and my mother, and then I will follow you." And he said to him, "Go back again, for what have I done to you?" So Elisha turned back from him, and took a yoke of oxen and slaughtered them and boiled their flesh, using the oxen's equipment, and gave it to the people, and they ate. Then he arose and followed Elijah, and became his* **servant** *(1 Kings 19:19-21).*

Hold on for a minute! I thought God said He was to anoint Elisha to be a prophet. But the Bible says Elisha rose up and became Elijah's servant. Here is the road for all fulfillment in ministry. You must always travel with the heart of a servant, an armorbearer. You will never fulfill your calling with any other attitude.

Jesus said, *"There is no greater love than to lay down one's life for one's friends"* (John 15:13 NLT). It is not difficult to claim we are submitted to Jesus, but the question is, are we submitted to another human being? That's a different story.

Here is another truth: *You are never really submitted to someone until you can submit when you disagree.* The purpose of this book is to minister healing between the leaders and the armorbearers, and to release a new revelation of relationship. It is a whole lot easier to yield to one another when we have done our best to establish some kind of relationship.

My pastor understood the calling and anointing on my life, and it was his desire to see that calling fulfilled. On the other hand, I understood my God-given duty to stand with my pastor and help him fulfill the vision God had given to both of us, and to fully submit myself to him.

There is a great fear today among many pastors that their associate ministers are out to steal the sheep from them. Some of that is insecurity of the pastor, but some of it is just flat true. As a result, there is little or no trust between the pastor and the armorbearers, no flow between them. I believe God has people prepared as armorbearers for every pastor and Christian leader. Someone to stand strong with you in the ministry, to complement and complete.

In the Kingdom of Jesus there are only Kingdom builders, not empire builders. Empire builders have built their ministry around themselves out of fear, or simply from ego. What will happen when an empire builder is gone? Empire builders are seasonal but Kingdom builders are generational.

Where would we be today if Jesus had not poured Himself into the twelve disciples? What would have happened if, on the day He

Armorbearers are
called to complete,
not compete.

ascended to the Father, there had been no one there to see Him go; no one to take up His ministry on earth?

Ask every pastor and spiritual leader this vital question: If you were taken off the scene today, where would your ministry be tomorrow? Most would have to admit that it would suffer. Jesus' ministry increased and multiplied because there were armorbearers standing with Him.

Armorbearer Definition

Before beginning a study of the actual Scriptures in which the word *armorbearer* appears, let's consider its original meaning, which must be firmly established if the true idea of the term is to be fully understood.

The word *armorbearer* is listed eighteen times in Strong's Concordance. All of the references are from the Old Testament. Each of these listings is referenced by two numbers, indicating that the word was originally translated from two Hebrew words.

As noted, the word *armorbearer* in the King James version of the Bible was translated from two Hebrew words. The first is *nasa,* or *nacah* (naw-saw). This is a primary word meaning "to lift." It has a great variety of applications, both figuratively and literally. Some of the more interesting applications are to: accept, advance, bear, bear up, carry away, cast, desire, furnish, further, give, help, hold up, lift, pardon, raise, regard, respect, stir up, yield. The second Hebrew word is *keliy* (kel-ee), which comes from the root word *kalah* (kaw-law), meaning "to end." Some of the applications of this root word are to: complete, consume, destroy utterly, be done, finish, fulfill, long, bring to pass, wholly reap, make clean, riddance.

From these two Hebrew words, we can see the duty of the armorbearer was to stand beside his leader to assist him, to lift him up, and to protect him against any enemy that might attack him. If we in the Church are not assisting, encouraging, and protecting our leaders, something is wrong.

Moving into Chapter 3, I talk about what pastors are looking for in armorbearers, and what the armorbearers are looking for in their leaders.

My prayer is that we all open our eyes to see how much God needs us to come together at this time and bring this revelation into the current culture.

When I examine my life right now, I'm not in the same place I was thirty years ago in ministry. I picked up my book one day and said, "Lord, am I still an armorbearer?" I heard a big, "Yes! You have just moved into a different position. You are not the armorbearer serving your pastor, you are now the armorbearer serving your city."

— 3 —

HOW TO
HONOR YOUR LEADER

We have now bathed ourselves in His wonderful forgiveness and we are now asking for an impartation of His Spirit, the armorbearer servant. Jesus is the Great Shepherd and His apostles began their ministry as His armorbearer servants. They served Him in every capacity, and we are being called to serve not only Jesus, but His leaders here on earth. Through serving His leaders we are serving Him. Jesus' disciples never questioned Him about how He was going to run His ministry. They just served.

This may seem like a heavy truth, but allow it to bypass your soul and go into your spirit where you are able to receive it. Honestly, you just have to commit to honor God through obeying His Word. It's okay to question God, it is *not* okay to be disobedient. For me it's always pretty simple. If God says it, then I am convinced that it is for my good. We have to receive God's Word as instructions to live by. I simply obey, knowing my true identity is as a son and not only a servant. It is my relationship with my

Father that causes me to rest in obedience. This truth sets us free from all the wounds and hurts and releases ministry once again.

By faith you have to step out and honor all authority. God directed us to do this in His Word, the Bible. I deal with authority in an upcoming chapter and my personal struggles I had to overcome to receive God's grace in this area. Submission to authority opens a path to pursue the calling God has placed in us, it teaches us to not constantly seek vindication when we release our wills and yield to His. Our soul is very demanding and it wants to reason and lead in its own way. But we have to yield ourselves to the infallible Scriptures and lay down our thinking at His feet and follow Him.

This book is all about an impartation, not just information. Take some time reading and absorbing these chapters and asking the Holy Spirit to minister to you. This teaching is what I have personally walked out in my life. It is a truth I live by today. There is an incredible joy in me right now because the Holy Spirit is coming upon you as you read this. You are being set free from all church hurt as you read through these pages.

Digest and meditate on these statements and allow the Holy Spirit to help you in your current environment. Take on God's way of doing things and you will end up with God results. You are a Kingdom child of God with a calling to fulfill, and Jesus is calling you to a higher level in your love walk with Him. Satan's assignment is broken and your giftings are flowing once again. The devil is afraid of you!

Now after we have discussed what a pastor needs from the armorbearer, we will then take a look at what the armorbearer

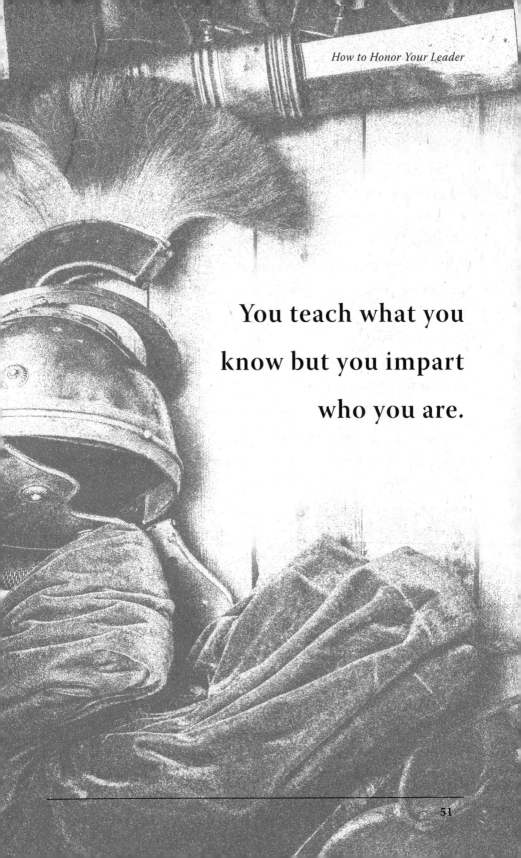

You teach what you
know but you impart
who you are.

needs from the leader. You are receiving this mandate, in training for the Jesus class of leader.

When I wrote the *God's Armorbearer* book series, I had been an associate for ten years. Writing this new one thirty years later, I have served as a pastor for ten years. I have lived on both sides, therefore I now can speak for the pastor *and* the armorbearer. My ministry spans more than forty years: twenty-seven of those years I was an associate pastor; six years were traveling as a teacher-evangelist; and ten as the lead pastor. I have seen it all—the good, the bad, and unfortunately, the ugly. I wish I could say it's all good, but it's not. Jesus is good and when I hang on to Him, I can walk through the ugly with His goodness all over me. Someone can be ugly, but I choose to pour out good.

Now let's examine this powerful Scripture: *"For the law was given through Moses, but **grace and truth came through Jesus Christ**"* (John 1:17). We all cry out for grace from Jesus. Thank God, Jesus ushered in His great grace and continues to pour it out. But it seems like we forget about the fact that Jesus came as grace *and* truth: Grace—Jesus loves everyone on the planet; Truth—no one gets into Heaven to be with the Father except through Jesus (John 14:6). Jesus, our Master, is saying, "I am all over you with grace, but the balance is that I am also here to instruct, lead, and correct through truth."

This current generation demands to be heard, while my generation demands to be honored. Now, I will take the lead as a pastor and sit down to listen. But all you God-inspired young pioneers, you young Christian warriors, devil destroyers, vision casters, and just flat smart ones, give honor to whom honor is due. What you honor comes to you and what you dishonor flees from you.

Honor has to be given whether we feel like the person deserves it or not. God Himself demands honor and then commands us to honor. If we do not honor God, He will always love us, but we shut our lives off from His grace. Now that truth is straight from Him:

> A son **honors** his father, and a servant his master. If then I am the Father, where is My **honor**? And if I am a Master, where is My reverence? Says the Lord of hosts to you priests who despise My name. Yet you say, "In what way have we despised Your name?" "You offer defiled food on My altar, but say, 'In what way have we defiled You?' by saying, 'The table of the Lord is contemptible.' And when you offer the blind as a sacrifice, is it not evil? And when you offer the lame and sick, is it not evil? Offer it then to your governor! Would he be pleased with you? Would he accept you favorably?" says the Lord of hosts (Malachi 1:6-8).

Honor means "deference, reverence, value at the highest degree. To give special recognition."

These men were using the blind and the lame as an offering to God on the altar. God said it is evil and cursed them for it. It is obvious we are releasing a curse on ourselves by dishonoring what He says to honor. We must take a close look at the spirit driving this culture into dishonoring authority, because God calls it evil.

The Holy Spirit commands us to give honor and we only receive from the gift that we honor. God is saying, "Where is My honor?"

Today many spiritual leaders are saying the same. By the way, there is a difference between honor and respect. Respect is an attitude, and honor is an action. My action toward God is to honor Him. I can respect God but give no honor and therefore cut Him out of my life. Some think, *I will honor God but I don't have to honor my leaders if I don't like them.* Really?

> *Dear brothers and sisters,* **honor those who are your leaders in the Lord's work.** *They work hard among you and give you spiritual guidance.* **Show them great respect and wholehearted love because of their work.** *And live peacefully with each other* (1 Thessalonians 5:12-13 NLT).

Anytime we read from God's Word, He is commanding—not suggesting. When we honor our spiritual leaders, we are honoring Him, so I honor as unto Him. That means get up and tell your leaders how much you love and appreciate them. Yield to their leadership. Brother Terry, are you teaching unconditional submission? No, I am not! I trust the Bible and I know there is a balance. If I am asked to do something that violates the Word of God, then I have a higher authority. But that is not usually the case. Let's take a deep breath and look at some Scriptures about honor. Let God speak, not me.

I know there are some pastors who may say, "Go get them, Pastor Terry. Tell them to submit or be condemned." Well, in a

God's Kingdom is
released through the
spirit of honor.

few minutes you may not being saying that. If I as a leader do not honor people who are God's children, then I will not receive honor.

Elders who do their work well should be respected and paid well, especially those who work hard at both preaching and teaching. For the Scripture says, "You must not muzzle an ox to keep it from eating as it treads out the grain." And in another place, "Those who work deserve their pay!" (1 Timothy 5:17-18 NLT)

Honor all people. Love the brotherhood. Fear God. Honor the king (1 Peter 2:17).

Husbands, likewise, dwell with them with understanding, giving honor to the wife, as to the weaker vessel, and as being heirs together of the grace of life, that your prayers may not be hindered (1 Peter 3:7).

Honor widows who are really widows (1 Timothy 5:3).

Children, obey your parents in the Lord, for this is right. "Honor your father and mother," which is the first commandment with promise: "that it may be well with you and you may live long on the earth" (Ephesians 6:1-3).

Be kindly affectionate to one another with brotherly love, in honor giving preference to one another (Romans 12:10).

Now to the King eternal, immortal, invisible, to God who alone is wise, be honor and glory forever and ever. Amen (1 Timothy 1:17).

I honor when:

- I ensure my spiritual leaders are blessed financially for the work they do.
- I ensure the people in the church and at my job know I love them and am available to help. Then I take them to lunch and pay, letting them witness my action of honor.
- I ensure my wife is taken care of and continually feels my love. I surprise her regularly with a gift of honor.
- I ensure the widows of the church are well taken care of.
- I ensure my children honor all authority, especially their mom and dad.
- I ensure God continually hears my voice of honor and praise!

This is the character of a true armorbearer of the Lord.

Let's look now from a leader's perspective about how an armorbearer can honor the leader. As a pastor you can bring me honor by understanding:

1. I'm your leader, but I'm not perfect.
2. I won't wake up in a good mood every day.

3. I won't always pat you on the back, but I do appreciate you.

4. I'd like to know you will pick up paper on the floor (sheep droppings) before the custodians come to clean, because that's what I do.

5. I expect you to conserve resources, as the church bills are always before my face.

6. I expect you to fulfill your responsibilities by the time I get to church.

7. I fully expect the care of this ministry to be yours also.

8. I understand you are a volunteer, but you volunteered for the Lord's army, not just mine.

9. I expect you to strive for excellence knowing you will not always achieve it; but if you don't strive for it, you will settle for mediocrity.

10. I expect you to love the people in the hard times because you represent me.

11. I expect you to be prepared for the unexpected at all times.

12. I expect you to pay attention when I am talking and please turn your cell phone off with it face down.

13. I need you to be my biggest cheerleader.

14. I need your prayers and support 24/7.

15. I need your support even when I am struggling in my attitude.

16. I need you to pray and watch over the care of my family.

17. I need you to be there at my call, and never be late.

18. I need your help by not complaining.

19. I need your love and for you to know I love you, even though you don't hear it enough.

20. I need you to be strong for me and allow me to lean on you at times.

21. I need you to handle it when I vent my frustrations.

22. I need your understanding when I am in the wilderness.

23. I need you to have complete confidence when you see the weakness in me.

24. I need you to truly and lovingly care for me and the flock.

25. I ask you to forgive me for any offense I have caused you. I am truly sorry. I need your forgiveness. Please honor me by forgiving me.

26. I need you to handle correction and confrontation from me without falling apart emotionally.

27. I need you to be the visionary in your own department and take full responsibility over it.

28. When a season of trials come to the ministry, I want to look to my side and see you standing there with me.

— 4 —

OUR HEAVENLY FATHER'S CRY TO HIS LEADERS

The cry from Millennials is one we need to take a moment and listen to. They accuse us of not listening, so why don't we get quiet and read what they have to say. Armorbearers really do want to serve us. We have asked them to honor us, so let's take the time to really hear what they are saying to us. Let's return the honor.

Here's the truth for leaders from the armorbearers' perspective. The armorbearer needs you to know:

1. I'm always there for you.
2. I don't need a thank you every time I help you, but a little appreciation goes a long way.
3. I'm willing to work overtime for you.
4. I'm daily praying for you.
5. I can handle your human side and not lose respect.

6. I truly desire to be your Timothy in the same way Timothy was to Paul, a true son in the faith.

7. I'd love to have some hang time with you. I promise not to allow familiarity.

8. I desire to have a relationship.

9. I may have been hurt in the past by leaders, but I'm willing to trust the Jesus in you.

10. I want you to speak the truth, not with hard words but in love.

11. I want you to know I can handle the truth because I'm looking for impartation.

12. I'm willing to be corrected, but not willing to have my spirit broken.

13. I want you to love me the same way you love yourself, in Jesus.

14. I don't mind doing difficult tasks, but please communicate to me how you want it accomplished.

15. Please delegate, not dictate.

16. I'm committed to follow your leadership.

17. I'm looking for you to do your best to model Jesus in front of me.

18. I want you as my leader to be comfortable in my presence.

19. I want you to trust me to do the things you don't like to do.

If Jesus were the pastor of a church, He would love the people whether they served Him or not.

20. I want you to know I will do my best to represent you well.

21. I want you to know I am dependable and I'll show up on time.

22. I can persevere through the hard times.

23. I desire you to be my spiritual father or mother.

24. I desire you to know how much I truly love you and am thankful to be working alongside you.

25. I need you to be transparent. If I don't know your heart, I can't strive for excellence for you. Your heart is more than just your vision to me.

26. Thank you for honoring me in the same manner that I honor you.

Let's remember grace and truth. The law came through Moses, but grace and truth came through Jesus. Here is an easy definition: *God gives you grace to walk in His truth.* The Lord sees the division between the generations. He feels the hurt of the Millennials and the Zs; He also feels the discouragement of the elder generation when the generations are attempting to connect with one another.

I want this chapter to touch deeply every leader and bring you hope for deep love and relational connection between you and your team. Throughout this chapter, remember that we are to model Jesus. You have to learn to live by what Zig Ziglar said, "Yesterday ended last night. Today is a brand-new day."

Jesus called all leaders to Himself. Does your team know the real you? Have you taught only the mechanics of leadership and not heart relationship? Jesus knew it had be taught, but more importantly *caught.*

We can't get angry at people when that's who we are called to influence for the Kingdom. One day when I was majorly frustrated I said, "Jesus, I know You died for all of them, but I'm not sure I can."

He said, "I understand your frustration, Terry, but I have no one else to love them through unless I love them through you." Now I'm going to be very vulnerable and share something that I'm going through. I have felt as though I have been in the deepest hole ever in my lifetime. When I got up this morning to write this chapter, I had no clue that I was going to share this. To be honest, I didn't know what I was going to do with this chapter. It's too personal and people wouldn't understand it, but here goes nothing, or everything. You may never pick up another book of mine because being this real is uncomfortable reading.

Here is the season in which I find myself: In less than one month, two of my elders resigned, who are good men that I leaned on heavily—as well as my children's pastor and then youth pastor shortly afterward. I thought I finally had a team I could flow with, then for no reason several families who had been with us for some time left the church. This impacted our finances in a very significant way as those who left were faithful tithers and leaders.

Now that was bad enough, but then in walks our oldest daughter who just had our first grandchild and she says, "Dad, I need to talk to you and Mom." She had been working with us for fifteen years.

She is just like me in so many ways, and Kim and I depended on her to be our right arm. She had experienced hurt in the church she grew up in, the place where Kim and I had served for quite a while. My heart began to beat quickly when she said, "Dad, the Lord has spoken to me to resign from your ministry and return to the place where I was hurt to be healed and restored."

"What are you are you going to do there?" I asked.

"Clean toilets if I need to."

As much as I knew it was God, and even though I was proud of her courage, the thought of not raising my granddaughter in my church was killing me. At this time in my life everyone seemed to be abandoning me. I was dying inside and didn't have a clue what to do.

I was ready to burn every leadership book I could get my hands on. None of it worked for me. I was waving the white flag. I was done, finished, through and wanted God just to take me home. I know I'm speaking to someone in this chapter right now. Your heart is breaking and you don't know what to do. Please hang on long enough to keep reading and wait for me to finish.

I know I'm not the best pastor in the world, but I also know I couldn't be the worst. Kim and I committed a long time ago that when people left the church, they would leave with my blessing. I always want to leave the door wide open for a return if it's possible. Boy, wouldn't it be good if we could pastor in our glorified bodies and then nothing would bother us. But unfortunately we can't! We have to deal with what happens and make it through. I was so low that low was looking down on me. Now that's just flat low.

Believe it or not, at the time of writing this, I haven't even shared this with my congregation. I may not have one after they read this. Well, me and old Job are good buddies. In one day everything was gone, so it seemed. I wasn't thinking about Job's restoration, I was only thinking about my pain. "Just stand up and speak to the mountain, Brother Terry!" I couldn't see it to speak to it because it was sitting on top of me. I needed someone to lift it for me. Man can't do it, but my Father the Mountain Mover can.

Desperate, I got up and went to the church and sat down in the foyer where I could look at a clock and watch time go by, know-ing that with every tick I was closer to Heaven. Not very spiri-tual, but that was where I was. Then I began to cry. From crying to moaning to wailing. There it was; the great dam that leads to brokenness. After a while, I told God I felt like Jehoshaphat. So immediately I felt in my heart to read the story. I turned to Second Chronicles 20:1-3:

> It happened after this that the people of Moab with the people of Ammon, and others with them besides the Ammonites, came to battle against Jehoshaphat. Then some came and told Jehoshaphat, saying, "A great mul-titude is coming against you from beyond the sea, from Syria; and they are in Hazazon Tamar" (which is En Gedi). And Jehoshaphat feared, and set himself to seek the Lord, and proclaimed a fast throughout all Judah.

The words jumped off the page into my heart—*"Jehoshaphat feared and set himself to seek the Lord"*! I sat for just a minute and then I had a conversation with my Father, "There is one thing I know how to do. I know how to seek You." He asked me, "What did you do when you were 21 years old, just married, your senior year of college with no chance of ministry anywhere?"

My mind went back to a field next to the apartment where I was living. I would get up at 5:15 every morning and meet with God from 5:30 a.m. to 6:45 a.m. Every day! He said to me, "Just make an appointment and keep it."

Since then much renewal has taken place. Every morning I have kept my appointment with Him. I have always been a man of prayer, but this is different. This is relationship building. Within a few weeks my new youth and children's pastor rose up from within the church. McCall and I meet weekly to pray for her future. I love that young woman more than ever. She will do incredible things for God.

In the middle of this season, I felt the nudge to rewrite *The Armorbearer*. I finally asked, "Father, am I to rewrite *God's Armorbearer* for the 30th anniversary of this book?" The answer was a big, "YES!" But I didn't expect to hear, "DO IT NOW!" So here we go! That took place on a Sunday morning. I was going to call Destiny Image Publishing on Monday to ask who my author representative was; I couldn't remember because it had been awhile since I had been in communication with them. Monday came and went and I didn't have time to make the call. But on Tuesday morning at 8 a.m. central time, after my appointment with God, I heard Him say, "Call now!" I did, and I waited for the receptionist to find the information.

God always gives
new revelation in
the middle of our
darkest hour.

Then suddenly Don Nori Jr. said hello. He is the president of Destiny Image, stepping into his father's position some time ago. I talked to his dad several times, but not Don Jr. He shared with me what the *Armorbearer* did for him years ago—how it changed his life. His dad handed the book to him and asked him to read it so he could faithfully follow his dad as an armorbearer. This was a divine appointment. What an encouragement it was for me to hear his testimony of what the *Armorbearer* meant to him, and his excitement about this new book.

Like Jehoshaphat's victory, my cry has turned to, "The Lord is good and His mercy endures forever!" My prayer is for every pastor who feels like waving the white flag, go back to your prayer closet. Make an appointment with God and start all over where you began. There is no book that can give you all the answers you are looking for right now. Only your Father can. Jesus reminded me of my calling:

> *Now it came to pass in those days that He went out to the mountain to pray, and continued all night in prayer to God. And when it was day, He called His disciples to Himself; and from them He chose twelve whom He also named apostles* (Luke 6:12-13).

I broke again one morning after reading that. My number-one calling is not to build a huge ministry. My calling is to Him. All the weight comes off when that is the revelation you commit to. I would love to give a testimony of a full restoration, but I have not seen it yet. But I have been restored in my heart, and that is what God wants to do for you now.

> *"Father! I lift up every pastor and leader who is facing a dark season in their lives. You are the great Restorer, and in Your hand is the power to deliver and set free. Let every leader feel Your warm embrace right now. Restore the joy of their salvation and let it come now, in Jesus' name!"*

Jesus has called you to Himself! Now let Him build your church. The supernatural power of the Holy Spirit is coming upon you now. You are greatly loved!

— 5 —

THE TRUE
ARMORBEARER...HELPS

*Now it came to pass in those days that He went out to
the mountain to pray, and continued all night in prayer
to God. And when it was day, He called His disciples to
Himself; and from them He chose twelve whom He also
named apostles* (Luke 6:12-13).

I dedicate this chapter to all the beautiful people who do all
the work behind the scenes in the local church. I am going
to speak directly to the local church. You may not even know
you are in a God-ordained office, but today you will discover that
you are indeed! You are the volunteer army that works night and
day giving of yourself to the Lord to serve and support your local
church. You are greatly beloved by God and your pastor.

I was up early in prayer this morning and suddenly I saw in my
spirit the Holy Spirit hovering over the waters as in Genesis. Then the
water turned into a mass of people. I asked the Lord, "Who is this?"

He said, "Those are all My children who serve, give, clean, teach, and support My Church. Terry, these are sometimes the overlooked army by humankind, but not by Me. These are the ones behind the scenes doing the work of ministry. I am sending a new anointing of refreshing upon them today."

Now before we go any deeper into this chapter, I speak the blessing of Abraham upon you (see Numbers 6:24-26): *"May the Lord bless you and keep you. May He cause His face to shine upon you, may He be gracious to you, may He lift up the light of His countenance upon you and may He give you peace in Jesus' name."* Wow! I feel the anointing coming from Heaven on you right now. He calls you His beloved. Your cry and your obedience have come up before Him. He rewards those who dedicate their lives for His Church.

I am writing this chapter on a Sunday morning, and the Lord wanted you to know you were on His heart. Please stand strong, be faithful, stay true to your calling. You are loved and needed by God and your pastor. The local church folds without you. God needs you to be strong!

The Father's love for the local church is more than you know! Rivers of refreshing are flowing from God to you now because just as Cornelius in Acts 10, you have come up as a memorial before Him today. I hear the Lord saying to you, "I need you to be strong for Me. I am sending revival rain on America. The harvest is plentiful, but the laborers are few. It's going to place a great demand on you. I need you to prepare yourself. I will use you in some unusual ways to service My harvest. Do not be overwhelmed when it happens. Stay in prayer to know what to do. But be ready for the work

The local church folds
without you. God
needs you to
be strong!

of ministry. At harvest time everyone will work to get the ripe harvest into the barn. I am coming upon you with My wisdom and releasing great grace. You are My hands and feet to bring them in. You must be ready to love, serve, and disciple them into the Kingdom of My dear Son. The Holy Spirit is coming upon you to complete the work. It will be fun not burdensome. Your pastor will need you more than ever," says the Lord of the harvest!

Now in Jesus' name I break off of you hurt, discouragement, anger, weariness, and neglect. I release strength, grace, and peace now to come from Heaven and invade your soul. You are God's harvester, His hands and feet for these last days. Be encouraged *now!*

Let's look at what the Bible says about the ministry of helps. This is where being an armorbearer begins:

For as the body is one and has many members, but all the members of that one body, being many, are one body, so also is Christ. ...For in fact the body is not one member but many. If the foot should say, "Because I am not a hand, I am not of the body," is it therefore not of the body?

And if the ear should say, "Because I am not an eye, I am not of the body," is it therefore not of the body? If the whole body were an eye, where would be the hearing? If the whole were hearing, where would be the smelling? But now God has set the members, each one of them, in the body just as He pleased. And if they were all one member, where would be the body be?

But now indeed there are many members, yet one body. And the eye cannot say to the hand, "I have no need of you"; nor again the head to the feet, "I have no need of you." No, much rather, those members of the body which seem to be weaker are necessary. And those members of the body which we think to be less honorable, on these we bestow greater honor; and our unpresentable parts have greater modesty, but our presentable parts have no need.

But God composed the body, having given greater honor to that part which lacks it, that there should be no schism in the body, but that the members should have the same care for one another. And if one member suffers, all the members suffer with it; or if one member is honored, all the members rejoice with it. Now you are the body of Christ, and members individually. And God has appointed these in the church: first apostles, second prophets, third teachers, after that miracles, then gifts of healings, helps, administrations, varieties of tongues (1 Corinthians 12:12,14-28).

Let's break down this Scripture passage into truths we can digest to see clearly what the Lord is saying to His local church.

1. The apostle Paul is comparing the natural body to the spiritual body of Christ.

The same way our physical body works is the same way the Body of Christ works. I am going to take this principle and show how the local church operates. The title of this portion of Scripture in my New Spirit-Filled Bible is "Unity and Diversity in One Body." The point is—why does the devil even have to bother fighting and oppressing the Body of Christ in so many places? He just sits back and watches while we destroy one another with our fighting and discord. That describes the condition of the local church that does not recognize its calling to love and unity. Remember, we are called to model God and walk in love like Jesus. Of course, I'm not talking about all local churches, but right now it seems that the Church as a whole is hanging on for dear life. We have to rediscover our purpose in the earth and begin to value one another.

2. The Body is not one member but many.

Thank God our physical body is not one big nose. We would sure look weird. But the local church is not one member either. Your gift is not more important than another gift. Those on the stage at times might be tempted to think they are the more important gift in the church. That is because I believe lucifer was a musician and an incredible orator and he became puffed up with pride. So the temptation is to feel more important. It has been said by a worship pastor, "If I didn't bring the anointing down through my music, where would this church be." Well, you are about to find out. Everyone is replaceable, including worship leaders and pastors. It's God's church and He can replace us if we get lifted up in pride.

The nose can't say to the eye, "I don't need you." What if the hands decided they didn't need the ears? Can you imagine your hands flapping on the side of your head because they are envious of the position of the ear and decided to steal the ears' place, to operate like the ear instead of flowing in their gifting? Now that would just be weird. The church cannot be weird and reach this world. Value your neighbor's part and God will place value on yours. I understood my part years ago and it helped me. I love worship, but I'm no musician. Maybe I can beg my musician friends to lay hands on me in an attempt to pass their gift to me, but that is just not going to happen. They will say, "Brother Terry, we love you, but it ain't there! You got no gift of music. Please stick to teaching." The sooner we learn this, the quicker will we will embrace unity. The result will be revival.

3. *God set each of us in the Body as He pleases.*

Wow! You and your unique gifting have been placed on this planet and in your church by God Himself. That knocks out all competition. That gives a wind of the Spirit the right to blow on your soul and release you to make a difference *together with others.* I cannot do my part without yours and you cannot do it without mine. But together we can fulfill God's purpose on earth and cause the local church to shine like Jesus. With all the fighting and discord in this world and hatred between nations, where is God's model of true love and unity on this planet? It is the local church! That is who we are. *We are to be the example of Heaven on earth.*

4. *For the members of the Body that seem to be less honorable, God bestows more honor.*

My wife, Kim, shared this one day and blew me away with this revelation. What are the inward, less honorable parts of the body?

The kidneys, liver, and all the guts. These are the parts we can't live without. We can live without hands, feet, a nose, ears, eyes, and other outward parts, but we can't live without our unseen parts. In the local church, I believe the outward parts are all the giftings that move in and about from the stage. At first glance, they might be seen by everyone to be the most important.

I know God has chosen the giftings, but when we look at it a different way we may be surprised who is rewarded in Heaven. The inward parts, I believe, represents the volunteers in the church whom no one sees—the nursery workers, greeters, parking lot attendants, ushers, and everyone else who behind the scenes keep the ministry going. They are generally not paid a salary but they serve from their heart. If you can relate to this right now, you will never know until you get to Heaven what you meant to your pastor and Jesus. You will be rewarded by Jesus Himself for doing your part in the local church and being a blessing to your pastor, which you certainly are.

5. The ministry of helps is an office called by God!

> Now you are the body of Christ, and members indi-
> vidually. And God has appointed these in the church:
> first apostles, second prophets, third teachers, after that
> miracles, then gifts of healings, helps, administrations,
> varieties of tongues (1 Corinthians 12:27-28).

The definition of this office is pretty simple. In the Greek, Hebrew, and every language on this planet, it is the one office that

Everyone is replaceable, including worship leaders and pastors.

defines itself in its title. It means H-E-L-P! I wish I had a loud-speaker to go off right now screaming, "Help!" Jesus needs you, your pastor needs you, and your church needs you to HELP! The harvest is calling for you to help!

Where I come from in the charismatic church circles, we think apostles are the coolest people on earth. If you're reading this from a fundamental denomination, please bear with me. The Bible very clearly recognizes the different gifts and offices Paul mentions in First Corinthians 12. Many other Scriptures also refer to these offices. I believe they are definitely operating in the earth today. So to make the point, I'm going to use some names that have influenced my life and are recognized as leaders in the charismatic Church. Now I need your imagination. Let's say I'm going to have a weeklong conference in Sherwood, Arkansas, and I'm going to invite the offices mentioned in this verse. I have put up a billboard of the names and faces who will be speaking every night. I have also plastered it all over social media. These are people who some today would call "big hitters." Announcements may say something like: "Speaking in Sherwood, Arkansas, on Monday night representing the office of the apostle is none other than Bill Johnson from Redding, California."

I can hear the people in Arkansas cheering right now. I may get calls from this chapter alone, asking when he is coming. That's how much we would love to have him here. "A present-day, recognized apostle is coming to Sherwood; Monday night's speaker is Bill Johnson. Tuesday night, are you ready? Prophet Kris Vallotton will be speaking." Oh man, I can't stand it. We are actually having a prophetic office in this city. "Tuesday night Kris will minister from his gifting and bless you through his spiritual insight." I have no clue right now where we are going to fit all the people. This is crazy. An apostle Monday night and a prophet Tuesday night. These offices are set up and called by God. The Bible says first apostles, then prophets.

"Okay everyone, take a deep breath because here comes Wednesday night! Teacher Mike Bickle from Kansas City International House of Prayer will be here. We are now loaded for a conference like no other. Some of the top charismatic leaders in the country will be in Sherwood. People are coming from all over the county. Ready for Thursday night? Miracle evangelist Todd White is confirmed for Thursday night in Sherwood!

"This office is called by God and set in the earth to impart God's heart to us. We all recognize the anointing in him and his love for the harvest and the miracles that follow him. Arkansas will never again be the same. Friday night is here and the healing ministry of Randy Clark from the Toronto Blessing will be here to pray for the sick. This state will experience the greatest awakening we have ever seen. WOW!"

Social media is going absolutely crazy over this combination of giftings and offices all in one week. Okay, I have barely made it through Friday night. I am so pumped that the anointing of the Holy Spirit is flowing through my veins by the impartation I have received.

"Now on the schedule for Saturday night right along up there with all these gifts is none other than Ike Gaynor. Now I know what you're thinking right now. Who on the planet is Ike? In the

Bible, God Jehovah put Ike's calling right in line with the rest of the greatest gifts and offices, and it's called HELPS!"

Obviously, I will have to get his permission to say all this, but Ike, for those who don't know him, is an usher in my church who stands in the ministry of helps and he makes me cry when I think of his faithfulness behind the scenes to serve me. One day I was mowing my yard, and he got angry and said, "Pastor, you will never mow your yard as long as I am around and able to do it." I didn't mean to take this much space to make this point, but you have to see that God puts helps, your calling and gift, right there with the ones we all admire.

Very few people make a fuss over the nursery workers when they come to church. I have never seen someone go to the nursery to get a new anointing. There are people at every service who are taken for granted, yet we never realize it. But thankfully God sees the inward parts that we think are less honorable and He bestows greater honor on them. The true honor will only be revealed at the judgment seat of Christ. Let the precious Holy Spirit wrap you now in His love to let you and all who serve know how much God loves you. He has called you and values you as His ministry of helps!

What He is saying to you is this, "I, your heavenly Father need your help. I need you to pray for My leaders. I need to you hold up my local church. I need you to be My disciple ready to disciple others. I need you to be faithful and I need you to stay in unity. I love you and I am sure proud of you!"

Signed,

God, your Father

— 6 —

AARON AND HUR— INNER CIRCLE ARMORBEARERS

I dedicate this chapter to the men and women who serve as associates, elders, and armorbearer teams who spend much of their time with their pastor—the inner circle armorbearers. This is the position of the twelve disciples who served Jesus. They did crowd control, handed out food, prayed for the sick, preached the gospel of the Kingdom, collected the leftovers from dinner, and heard the inside scoop of what Jesus was really thinking. What's cool is that the Holy Spirit lets us listen in on their conversation every time we read His Word, the Bible.

What we don't know exactly is all the time Jesus invested in them from day to day. They walked in an incredible relationship with Him. Your office as an associate, inner-circle armorbearer, or elder is one of the most important offices in the local church—because you represent your leader everywhere you go.

I believe that every person in the Body of Christ and leader should carry an armorbearer spirit, and I teach that. But I also know that in the local church there are those called by God to serve their leader in an inner circle for the sake of ministering to the Body. I fulfilled that office for twenty-seven years in three different churches. Now before anyone gets upset about that statement, thinking that pastors have cliques, let's stop and look at Jesus and how He operated.

Now after six days Jesus took Peter, James, and John his brother, led them up on a high mountain by themselves (Matthew 17:1).

And He permitted no one to follow Him except Peter, James, and John the brother of James (Mark 5:37).

Now as He sat on the Mount of Olives opposite the temple, Peter, James, John, and Andrew asked Him privately (Mark 13:3).

And He took Peter, James, and John with Him, and He began to be troubled and deeply distressed (Mark 14:33).

When He came into the house, He permitted no one to go in except Peter, James, and John, and the father and mother of the girl (Luke 8:51).

Jesus' leadership style was pretty clear on building an inner circle. These were the ones who would see His humanity more than anyone else. The problem with us is, Jesus was without sin and we are not. Our humanity is a mess sometimes and the insecurity of that tries to rule in our leadership. As pastors we almost trust no one. That is why God gives His leaders an inner-circle team of armorbearers who will hold true to the integrity of your office. Sometimes people don't understand the loyalty of an armorbearer and criticize you for being discreet and loyal. But what you know could hurt the pastor if revealed.

Please understand I am not talking about leaders who live in defiance of the Bible. They are false and should be exposed. Paul dealt severely with leaders who misrepresented the gospel of the Kingdom. But most men and women of God are holding up a standard as best they can. They depend on those around them to be Aarons and Hurs, to hold up their arms while smelling the BO of their humanity. It ain't pretty sometimes.

I always thought I would be the perfect pastor because of all the years I served as an armorbearer and associate; but to my surprise, not everybody is crazy about my personality and way of doing things. Though as an inner-circle armorbearer, you are called to a higher standard. You must hold the confidentiality of your leader. I am going to lay this out as a list of must and must-not suggestions. I lived these standards for more than twenty-seven years to be a support to my leader, to be someone he could lean on when he was weary. I heard his heart cry for help and did my best before Jesus to be there for his success, not mine.

There is a call for Aarons and Hurs. There is a call for the Peters, Jameses and Johns in inner-circle ministry. They all started as armorbearers for their leaders, serving in whatever capacity they were asked. As a staff pastor, it's not about how you can shine, it's about your leaders and how they shine. Now if that sounds hard, I'm sorry. But it's still the truth. Team or no team, someone still has to lead. My job as the armorbearer was to see to it that the leader was taken care of. Believe me, Peter, James, and John knew who was in charge; and the rest of the disciples knew who was in Jesus' inner-circle. The real victory comes when we stop trying to compete for some inner circle. Serve Jesus and serve your leader, and let God exalt you.

A man of God said this to me and I live by it: *What you fight to get you lose, and what you release will come to you.* So stop fighting for some position or title and start serving with the heart of Jesus, the Chief Armorbearer, Servant-Follower, and Leader.

The "Musts" of an
Inner Circle Armorbearer

1. You must be the Aaron and the Hur for your leader.

*So Joshua did as Moses said to him, and fought with Amalek. And Moses, Aaron, and Hur went up to the top of the hill. And so it was, **when Moses held up his hand, that Israel prevailed**; and when he let down his hand,*

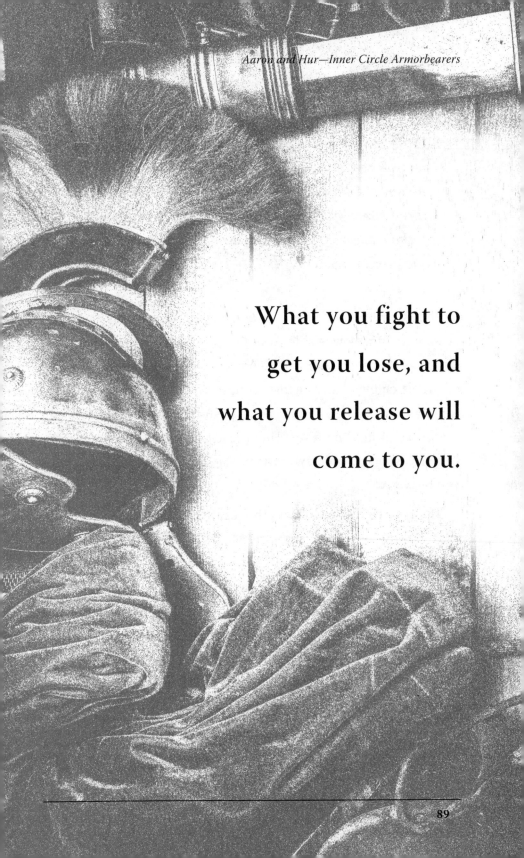

What you fight to
get you lose, and
what you release will
come to you.

> *Amalek prevailed. But **Moses' hands became heavy;** so they took a stone and put it under him, and he sat on it. And **Aaron and Hur supported his hands, one on one side, and the other on the other side; and his hands were steady** until the going down of the sun. So Joshua defeated Amalek and his people with the edge of the sword* (Exodus 17:10-13).

This story tells us that Moses got tired holding up his arms. But as long as Moses was able to hold up his hands, Joshua and his army were winning the battle. As soon as he dropped his arms, the battle changed and he lost ground. I believe this scenario represents the call of God and vision a pastor carries. Sometimes you get weary of holding it up. That could be your fault because you will not delegate, which was the problem Moses was dealing with and he was wearing himself out.

Then when Moses' strength began to fail, Aaron and Hur provided the necessary support. Moses didn't ask them for help when he was struggling, but they saw what was happening and then quickly went to help—they went into action. They provided Moses with a place to sit and they held up his arms. The story tells us that they found a rock and placed it under him so he could sit down. They did not take Moses to the rock, they brought the rock to Moses. And then they stood beside him, supporting his arms, keeping the staff of God lifted up. Moses did not have to say, "Aaron and Hur, come up here, I am struggling." No. They were there with him, and when they saw him struggle, they provided the necessary help without being asked. They didn't ask Moses, "Is there anything we can do?"

In the inner circle you must have eyes to see when your leader is weary. You don't have to ask to help, you just do it. Many a day I went to my pastor and said, "I know you're struggling with something and I'm here to relieve you of it if you will let me." I also made it my mandate to try to take him out to lunch once a month and pay for it. He always paid for lunch whenever he was out with staff, but I wanted him to feel what it was like for someone to pay for his meal. A simple but refreshing gesture of kindness to him, and me. We kept our relationship strong during some of the storms of ministry.

The name Aaron means "light bringer" and Hur means "liberty." That's who a pastor needs on his or her inner-circle team, Mr. Light Bringer and Mr. Liberty!

2. You must always provide strength for your leader.

By your very presence, a true armorbearer will always display and produce an attitude of faith and peace. If you are to be successful in service as an armorbearer to your pastor, he must sense the joy and victory which are integral parts of your lifestyle. That alone will minister to him. It is a great relief to the pastor to know that he does not have to carry his assistant physically, mentally, and spiritually. Many times I have seen pastors drained physically and emotionally because their associate was always in need of something. Your pastor has plenty of sheep to take care of; he doesn't need to feel you as a weight. Pastors will carry a special love for their inner circle, as it was obvious that Jesus did for His three. But you should be assisting him, giving him much-needed rest in mind and body by demonstrating that your faith is strong and active. Someone told me one day, "Just fake it till you make it." My wife always says, "No, you must *faith* it until you make it." There is no other way to live. Sometimes you are going to have to act in faith so that your leader can be encouraged. The Bible says, *"Let the weak say, 'I am strong'"* (Joel 3:10).

3. You must have a deep-down sense of respect for your leader, and acceptance for and tolerance of the leader's personality and way of doing things.

God made us all different. At least 50 percent of the time, your pastor's way of doing things will differ from yours. That difference should not be allowed to cause a problem for you or your spiritual leader.

When I served as an associate pastor, I learned a secret that helped me flow in harmony with my leader. I determined that if the end result of my pastor's plan is to build and extend the Kingdom of God and win souls for Jesus, then I would be willing to flow with the plan. Our goal is the same, our methods are different. So what does it really matter whose methods are used, as long as the goal is reached? I stopped fighting for a certain method and looked at the goal. I was not the one with final authority and the buck did not stop with me. So when the decision from my pastor was to wait on a matter, I let it go for the right timing.

I'm a fighter when I feel I'm right, but the Lord taught me the power of humility. You don't get the right to fight for right just because you think you're right. Am I right or am I right? On this point I know I am right. Submit, stay humble, and let Jesus exalt you—because in any and every conflict He is always right. If you will adopt this attitude toward your pastor, there will be a knitting of hearts between the two of you. He will know that you are not there to argue with him or to challenge his decisions, but that you are there to work with him in achieving his God-given objectives.

4. You must instinctively understand your leader's thoughts.

"For I have no one like-minded, who will sincerely care for your state" (Philippians 2:20). That's what Paul said about Timothy. I can hear what you are probably thinking right now: *My pastor and I just don't think alike.* That's right; no two people do. And that is one of the problems that must be dealt with in being an inner circle armorbearer. Amos 3:3 says, *"Can two walk together, unless they are agreed?"* Now how do we explain that Scripture? Here is what I feel from the Holy Spirit: We will never totally agree on method, but we must always agree on vision. Remember, two visions equal division!

The disciples were with Jesus for three long years and yet they did not begin to think as He thought until after He had died, was buried and resurrected, ascended into Heaven, and received the Holy Spirit. Just as God's Spirit was eventually imparted to these men, after a period of time your pastor's spirit will come upon you, and the two of you will become like-minded. You will begin to walk in an impartation and not just a head full of information. You will take on his spirit as you spend more time in his presence.

Trust will be built and his heart for ministry will become your heart for ministry.

5. *You must make the advancement of your leader your most important goal.*

I asked the Lord, "What about my dreams and goals, and the vision You have placed in my heart?" He said to Me, "Son, you are not to live for the fulfillment of your dreams or vision. Set it as your goal to achieve your pastor's dreams, the vision of the house, and I will make sure that yours are fulfilled." Again, what you make happen for others, God will make happen for you! That is the law of the Kingdom and the royal law of love.

6. *An armorbearer must possess endless strength so as to thrust, press, and force his way onward without giving way under harsh treatment.*

"For what credit is it if, when you are beaten for your faults, you take it patiently? But when you do good and suffer, if you take it patiently, this is commendable before God" (1 Peter 2:20). This passage makes it very clear that there will be times in the midst of battle when you and I will feel that we are being wrongfully treated. These types of situations are bound to arise, but do not allow satan to put resentment into your heart. Learn to give the situation over to the Lord and endure what comes patiently; God will be pleased with you.

It may be that in your heart you know you made the right decision. But in the eyes of your leader, it may seem wrong. Such times will develop character in you, if you will walk in love, allowing

Your inner-circle armorbearers today will be pastors and leaders tomorrow.

the Spirit of God to take charge of the matter; your strength will always come by encouraging yourself in the Lord, as David did in First Samuel 30:6.

The easy thing to do is say, "Well, no one around here appreciates me; I was rebuked and I know I was right in what I did." Do not give in to the flesh. Get in prayer and stay there until First Peter 2:20 has become part of your very being. Having a good attitude during correction time will build Christ's character in you. This is learned in the hard times, because you *will* be rebuked at times by your leader. Welcome to the inner circle. You cannot wear your emotions on your sleeve. Someone said this and it's a great statement: *You can't let your emotions drive the car, but you can't put them in the trunk either. They are part of you. You have to place them in the passenger seat of your life and deal with them. They will fight to drive but if ever allowed in the driver's seat, they will destroy your call. They will scream when hurt, they will pout when they don't get their way and they will get angry when they are rebuked.*

I am probably hitting a major vein right now.

You know what I did in the twenty-seven years of being an associate? Whether I was right or wrong, the Lord gave me a promise: "Terry, always take the high road and humble yourself and I will exalt you and vindicate if necessary." Sometimes the Lord just said, "Shut up and submit." I'm sorry if that offends you, but that is the way He talks to me. I can be stubborn. Jesus rebuked the unbelief of the disciples, scolded them when they failed to cast out a devil, told them all to leave if they wanted to, and made no promise of security for them. But man, did He love them and was totally committed to father them. Rebuke, correction, and instruction is part of the package. I wish it was always done in love, but it won't be. You have to know that. You work with people who have clay feet. If that bothers you, then look down at your own.

7. An armorbearer must follow orders immediately and correctly.

In order to be a good leader, you must be a good follower. And being a good follower means taking care of things quickly and efficiently. If you aspire to become a leader, then the one you serve today must be able to depend upon you to carry out his directives. The following are some simple keys to help you to become a better armorbearer:

- First, write down the orders of your leader just as a waiter writes down an order for food. Make sure your leader gets exactly what he ordered. You're probably thinking, *Boy, what a revelation!* But let's be practical. God had everything written down for us so we would not forget anything. We dare not do any less for ourselves.

- Second, ask your leader to explain anything you don't understand. Make sure you have the correct information before you leave to carry out the order. Many times we misrepresent our leader because we misunderstand what he means.

- Third, treat his orders as your highest priority. When asked to do something, do it immediately! I am always blessed when my secretary is efficient. Her efficiency ministers to me. The same results will come when you put your heart into carrying out instructions quickly and correctly.

Once a directive is given, then within twenty-four hours let your leader know what is going on. "It's finished" or "Here is the progress" of the task. Here is my BIG "never" to my team—never come into my office telling me about a problem unless you have three solutions ready to solve it. And I get to choose which one. Anyone can say there is a leak in the dam. The ministry is falling. Your leader needs Aaron and Hur to come and reveal the *light* that will set the congregation and your pastor *free*. Where the Spirit of the Lord is there is liberty!

— 7 —

ARMORBEARERS OF THE OLD TESTAMENT

A good example of the loyalty of an armorbearer is found in the story of the death of Abimelech (Judges 9:45-55). This event took place during a war in which Abimelech was laying siege to a city. He was succeeding in his attempt to seize the city and had the enemy on the run. When he came to a tower where many of the people had taken refuge, he was prepared to burn it down. As wood was being laid at the foot of the tower, a woman in the top threw down a piece of millstone which struck Abimelech on the head, cracking his skull.

He called to his armorbearer and ordered the young man, *"Draw your sword and kill me, lest men say of me, 'A woman killed him'"* (Judges 9:54). Even though Abimelech was wicked, the loyalty of his armorbearer is obvious. He was the closest person to the king when the stone struck him on the head. He was just as concerned about Abimelech's tainted honor as Abimelech was himself. He did not want it said that his officer had been killed by a woman. His instant obedience is also recorded: *"So his young man thrust him through, and he died"* (Judges 9:54).

Saul's Armorbearer

In First Samuel 31:4-6 and First Chronicles 10:4-5, we find another account of an officer at war, his armorbearer at his side. Saul and his army were fighting against the Philistines and were losing ground. Saul's army, realizing that defeat was imminent, turned to flee. His men, including his three sons, were killed and Saul was wounded by arrows.

He turned to his armorbearer and ordered him, *"Draw your sword, and thrust me though with it, lest these uncircumcised men come and thrust me through and abuse me"* (1 Samuel 31:4). Saul wanted to die at the hands of his armorbearer rather than be captured and tortured by the enemy. However, his armorbearer would not oblige him, so Saul took his own life by falling on his sword. *"And when his armorbearer saw that Saul was dead, he also fell on his sword, and died with him"* (1 Samuel 31:5).

There are many things revealed in this portion of Scripture. At some point in the battle, Saul's forces turned to flee. His army was put to defeat, his men killed. Later in the chase, his three sons were slain. The enemy came close enough to wound Saul. That was when he turned to his armorbearer and made his request to die at his hands.

Note that although everyone else had fled, leaving Saul to face the whole enemy army alone, his faithful armorbearer was right alongside him. Saul, being the king, rode on the back of the fastest horse or in the swiftest chariot. If he traveled by chariot, then his armorbearer was his driver. If he went on horseback, then Saul's horse must have been chosen by his armorbearer because it was part of his duty to select and care for his officer's mount, equipment, and supplies. Needless to say, the armorbearer's horse had to be of equal strength, speed, and stamina as his master's. The armorbearer could be trusted to choose and select for his officer because he knew how his commander thought and what he liked and needed.

Through all the fighting and fleeing, Saul's armorbearer had managed to dodge the arrows and stay alongside his leader. When Saul commanded his faithful servant to thrust him through with his sword, *"but his armorbearer would not, for he was greatly afraid"* (1 Samuel 31:4).

It seems peculiar that an armorbearer would be so afraid; he had been selected, trained, and prepared to serve in battle. Because he was an armorbearer to the king, he was probably more skilled in warfare than any other soldier in the king's army. His duty was to protect the commander in chief. It doesn't seem logical that a man who was trained and prepared to give his life to save and defend the king would be afraid.

In the Hebrew, this word translated "afraid" in the King James Version is *yar* (yaw-ray). It does not mean to fear in the sense of being frightened or terrorized, but to fear out of reverence! In this case, it means to greatly respect and honor. Now the armorbearers reaction is much more understandable. This man had spent all his time in Saul's service, caring for and protecting him. His entire reason for being was the preservation of the life of the king. If there was even the slightest chance that Saul could be saved from destruction, then he had to take that chance, regardless of the odds against its success.

Perhaps it was just too much to ask the man who had protected Saul all this time to take the very life he was pledged to defend. He just could not bring himself to destroy the person he had spent his life preserving and protecting.

Notice the reaction of Saul's armorbearer contrasted with that of Abimelech's servant who did kill his officer when ordered to do so. Here we see two different reactions from two men who had dedicated and sacrificed their lives to the welfare of their superiors. Perhaps the reason their reactions were different is because the circumstances were different. Although Saul had been severely wounded by arrows, perhaps his armorbearer did not judge his wounds to be fatal. The young man was probably trained in attending to battle wounds. Perhaps he would have preferred to try to outrun the Philistines and hide somewhere, so he could nurse Saul back to health.

On the other hand, Abimelech had been hit on the head with a large piece of millstone, and his skull had been crushed. The wound was probably not very pretty. Perhaps the contents of his skull were coming out of the wound. Death seemed inevitable. Saul said, *"Draw your sword and thrust me through, lest these uncircumcised men come and thrust me through and abuse me."*

Abimelech said, *"Draw your sword and kill me, lest men say of me, 'A woman killed him.'"*

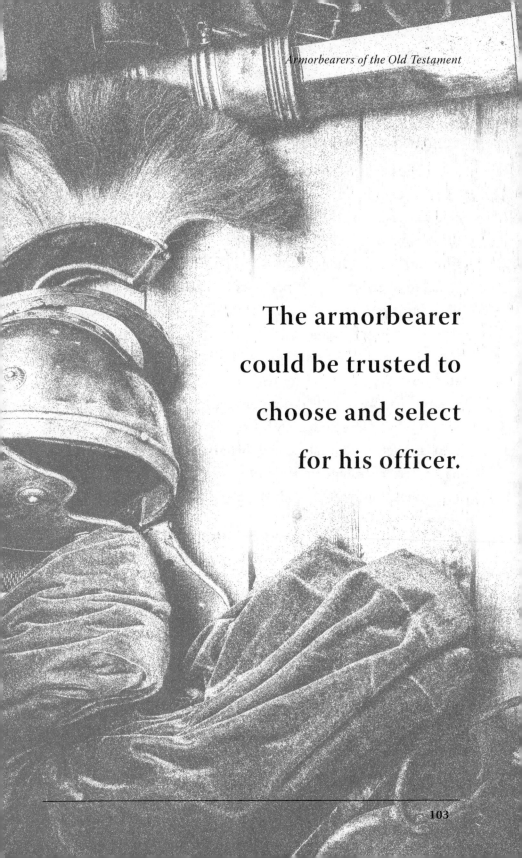

The armorbearer
could be trusted to
choose and select
for his officer.

The difference is that Abimelech was dying; Saul was not. Saul simply feared that the Philistines would come and torture him.

Perhaps Saul's armorbearer would rather have tried to escape with his commander, or maybe even to fight to the death alongside him. But one thing is for sure—out of respect, he could not be the one to put an end to Saul's life. It was a sense of reverential fear, respect and honor, not fright that caused the armorbearer to fail to obey his king. When Saul realized that his armorbearer would not comply with his request, he fell on his own sword. In true armorbearer fashion, as a man who had spent his whole life following Saul, the armorbearer knew that this was no time to stop now. When his master fell on his own sword and ended his life, the armorbearer had no more reason to live. Out of respect for his officer, he also fell on his sword. Suicide had not been his idea. In fact, if Saul had asked, his armorbearer may have even had a better strategy or a plan to escape from the hands of the Philistines. But since Saul chose to end his life, so did his faithful servant.

Jonathan's Armorbearer

In First Samuel 14:1-23 there is another account of a relationship between a young man and his armorbearer. Jonathan ordered his armorbearer to accompany him to the garrison of the Philistines against whom he and the other Israelites were warring. He wanted to go over secretly; Jonathan had not told his father, Saul, of his intentions. Though the king knew nothing about the plan, and though he and his master were only two against an entire army, Jonathan's armorbearer obeyed.

In First Samuel 14:6, Jonathan says, *"Come, let us go over to the garrison of these uncircumcised; it may be that the Lord will work for us. For nothing restrains the Lord from saving by many or by few."* The young and fearless armorbearer answers, *"Do all that is in your heart. Go then; here I am with you, according to your heart."* As the two young men climbed up toward the enemy's camp, God confirmed to them that He had, in fact, delivered the enemy into their hand. Jonathan turned to his companion and said, *"Come up after me..."* (1 Samuel 14:12 AMPC).

When Jonathan and his armorbearer reached the place where the enemy was standing, *"they fell before Jonathan. And as he came after him, his armorbearer killed them"* (1 Samuel 14:13.) The passage goes on to explain how God saved the whole nation of Israel that day, through the brave actions of Jonathan and his faithful, obedient armorbearer.

It is curious to note that Jonathan said, *"It may be that the Lord will work for us."* Although Jonathan was not certain about what would happen, his armorbearer was more than willing to follow. His answer in verse 7 reveals the proper attitude of any armorbearer, *"Do all that is in your heart. Go then; here I am with you, according to your heart."* The Amplified Bible says it this way: *"Do everything that is in your heart (mind); here I am with you in whatever you think [best]."* The New International Version says, *"Do all that you have in mind. Go ahead; I am with you heart and soul."* The Good News Version: *"Whatever you want to do, I am with you."*

The Living Bible: *"Fine! Do as you think best; I'm with you heart and soul, whatever you decide."*

As they approached the enemy, Jonathan's armorbearer knew his place. He was to come after Jonathan. In verse 13 we see that it was the anointing upon Jonathan, the anointing of a leader that caused the enemy to fall. The young armorbearer was diligent to follow along after his officer, destroying the enemy who had been knocked to the ground by God's anointing upon his leader: *"and his armorbearer killed them"* (1 Samuel 14:13).

This is a classic example of the humility and diligence of a biblical armorbearer. He wins victories and slays enemies while his leader gets the glory; one who trusts his officer, even in what may appear to be a whim; one who takes his place behind the person he serves, not striving to get out in front.

David as Armorbearer

In First Samuel 16:14-23 we find the story of the last of the five armorbearers. King Saul was troubled. He had a distressing spirit, so he decided to find a skillful musician who could ease his oppressed state of mind. A young man was recommended to the king by one of his servants: *"Look, I have seen a son of Jesse the Bethlehemite, who is cunning in playing, and a mighty man of valor, a man of war, prudent in speech, and a handsome person; and the Lord is with him"* (1 Samuel 16:18).

David, the young man, was sent to Saul, bearing gifts. We are told that Saul *"loved him greatly"* and made him his armorbearer

(1 Samuel 16:21). He could minister strength to Saul, causing him to feel *"refreshed and well"* (1 Samuel 16:23).

Verse 18 describes the young armorbearer as a:

- Skillful musician
- Mighty man of valor
- Man of war
- Person prudent in speech
- Handsome man in appearance
- Person the Lord was with

All of these qualities are biblical descriptions of a true armorbearer.

Perhaps the fact that David had once been Saul's armorbearer further explains his attitude when he later declared that he would not touch or harm *"the Lord's anointed"* (1 Samuel 26:9.) No matter how hard Saul tried to kill David, and no matter how many opportunities David had to slay Saul, David never struck back.

Did David walk in the same fear that caused Saul's future armorbearer to refuse to kill him? More than likely. This respect and honor toward God's anointed may also explain David's attitude of extreme repentance, sorrow, and humility before Saul after he had sneaked up behind the king in a cave and cut off the edge of his robe (1 Samuel 24:1-6). David was a true armorbearer, one who held no grudges and faithfully and obediently withstood his captain's harsh treatment. The result was his own eventual promotion to a place of high respect and honor.

In these Old Testament examples we witness armorbearers giving their lives for their leaders. It was an honor for them to be chosen for such a duty. They were handpicked to be the greatest of warriors to guard the king. It is this spirit that is to be restored into ministry today. God is picking the greatest warriors to guard His servants in honor to the King.

God is picking the
greatest warriors to
guard His servants in
honor to the King.

THE CHARACTERISTICS OF AN ARMORBEARER

As leaders we have to ask ourselves, "What are we looking for in an armorbearer?" We need God to send us men and women who can receive from us and stay faithful to our vision. I am going to list some character traits that we can look for in our leadership team. As an armorbearer, I would ask you to measure your heart by these attributes, because leaders are looking for these traits in the people they want to work beside.

Armorbearer Traits

1. Armorbearers are willing to pour water over the hands of their leader.

This trait became a real revelation to me while I was on a mission trip in Africa in the absolute bush—where I imagined Tarzan and Jane lived. Mike Croslow, who is one of my dearest friends had invited me to go with him and minister with a group of churches for three days. It was on the border of Tanzania and Uganda. What a trip that was! It was crazy the things we saw God do, but it was difficult to stay out there at night.

I was preaching the first day with two interpreters, in two languages, and trying to remember my last point by the time it got back to me. God moved in spite of all the challenges. I had preached for two hours and was ready for lunch. There were no modern kitchens—it was banana leaves in a hole over charcoal and an open fire. The pastors escorted me to a small church and sat me down beside Mike for lunch.

We had been preaching out in the open under a tree because of the crowds. As I sat there they brought out a big pot of soup and some stuff called millet. I call millet playdough with gravel. It is very thick and grainy.

I looked at Mike and said, "Where are the utensils?"

He laughed and said, "Your hands are your utensils." I looked at him puzzled because I didn't understand how to eat soup with my hands. One of the African pastors laughed and showed me what to do. He took the thick millet and rolled it into a ball and with his thumb made a hole in the middle of it. Then he proceeded to dip it into the soup. Pretty simple, but just not the way I am used to eating soup.

Right before I started eating, a young man walked in with a bar of soap and a pitcher of water. He asked me to hold out my hands and he washed them. Then I was ready to eat. I spent three days there and loved every minute of it. They were some of the most beautiful people on the planet. They gave us such incredible honor. About two weeks after returning home, I was reading Second Kings in my morning devotional when I came across this Scripture:

> *But Jehoshaphat said, "Is there no prophet of the Lord here, that we may inquire of the Lord by him?" So one of the servants of the king of Israel answered and said, "Elisha the son of Shaphat is here, who poured water on the hands of Elijah"* (2 Kings 3:11).

Suddenly, *"Elisha who poured water on the hands of Elijah"* jumped off the page. My mind went to Uganda and that young man who poured water on my hands. He was a servant to me the same way Elisha was to Elijah. The culture in Africa is the same in many Middle Eastern countries. They do not eat with a fork and spoon, they eat with their hands.

How many years have we preached about receiving a double portion on our lives just like Elisha did though Elijah. Everybody I know wants a double portion and anointing for ministry, but no one really has a clue how to get it. It comes only to those who are willing to pour water over the hands of their leaders through servanthood. Elisha cooked Elijah's meals, did his laundry, heard his complaints, and did whatever Elijah asked of him. Tradition said the service of Elisha to Elijah was probably between fifteen to twenty years. I will guarantee that Elijah was not easy to work for. I am sure Elisha at times felt like pouring water on his head and not his hands. That's crazy to think about.

Do you want a double portion? I hear a shout! "Oh yes, Jesus! Come lay it on me." Well, here is the next question. If you really want a double portion of the anointing, are you willing to pick up water and pour it over the hands of your leader in servanthood through good times, hard times, and challenging times? Now, I think you might think twice before asking for a double portion.

I was teaching on this very thing one day and the Lord spoke something to my heart, "Terry, when it came time for Elijah to go, who was the person Elijah asked, 'What do you want from me?'" Then I heard the Lord speak clearly, "Terry, it was the one carrying the water." Elisha gave himself to Elijah and that, and that only, made him the candidate for the double anointing.

The young leaders who are looking to pour water on your hands are your armorbearers and potential spiritual sons and daughters. The ones who have their own agenda and do not carry your vision are not. That's how you tell who the real armorbearers are.

2. Armorbearers are faithful in the small things.

> Now the Lord said to Samuel, "How long will you mourn for Saul, seeing I have rejected him from reigning over Israel? Fill your horn with oil, and go; I am sending you to Jesse the Bethlehemite. For I have provided Myself a king among his sons."
>
> Thus Jesse made seven of his sons pass before Samuel. And Samuel said to Jesse, "The Lord has not chosen these." And Samuel said to Jesse, "Are all the young men

here?" Then he said, "There remains yet the youngest, and there he is, keeping the sheep." And Samuel said to Jesse, "Send and bring him. For we will not sit down till he comes here." So he sent and brought him in. Now he was ruddy, with bright eyes, and good-looking. And the Lord said, "Arise, anoint him; for this is the one!" Then Samuel took the horn of oil and anointed him in the midst of his brothers; and the Spirit of the Lord came upon David from that day forward. So Samuel arose and went to Ramah (1 Samuel 16:1,10-13).

Wow! Don't you just love that? All the brothers were rejected and here was the youngest out keeping the sheep and he gets God's attention and is anointed king. The Lord made it clear He looks on the heart and not the title. That gives every one of us hope that God can use you to shake your places of influence. He doesn't need your name to make Him great, He only needs your armorbearer heart to do it. As I read that one day, the Holy Spirit asked me a question, "What did David do that day after he was anointed to be king?" I knew the answer when asked. He went back to the shepherd's field to keep the sheep. There is where he proved the anointing of God by killing a lion and a bear under the eyes of God and no one else.

You will be proven faithful under God's eyes first, and not your leader's eyes. Now when you examine this story closely, you have to ask, "Why didn't Jesse bring David in with the rest of the brothers? Why did Samuel have to ask Jesse if there were any more sons?" The reason is that Jesse didn't think that much of David who was the runt of the litter.

The way God selects leaders and the way we select leaders is different. God looks for armorbearers who are willing to serve. Before David faced Goliath he told Saul,

> *Then David said to Saul, "Let no man's heart fail because of him; your servant will go and fight with this Philistine." And Saul said to David, "You are not able to go against this Philistine to fight with him; for you are a youth, and he a man of war from his youth." But David said to Saul, "Your servant used to keep his father's sheep, and when a lion or a bear came and took a lamb out of the flock, I went out after it and struck it, and delivered the lamb from its mouth; and when it arose against me, I caught it by its beard, and struck and killed it. Your servant has killed both lion and bear; and this uncircumcised Philistine will be like one of them, seeing he has defied the armies of the living God"* (1 Samuel 17:32-36).

He was basically saying, "Saul, I have been faithful over my father's sheep and God has proven Himself to me. The same God who delivered me from the bear and the lion will be the same God who uses me to kill Goliath." I believe in the risk of faith. Faithfulness in the small things produces the faith when you face your Goliath. Promotion never comes without risk. You spell faith—RISK! As an armorbearer you have the heart of God; and when the time comes, you will have His faith also.

When I was twenty-two years old, I started in full-time ministry. I remember the day I sat in my pastor's office and he looked at me and asked, "Terry, what are your talents?" Man! I thought, *Dear Lord, I just got here and I'm going to get fired. I don't have any talents to think of.* So the first thing in my mind was, *I will be faithful, loyal, and I will never be late.* I didn't realize at the time that was what the pastor needed to hear. So on I went into ministry. I was green but had a heart to learn.

My first day on the job in 1979, I met my pastor at 8 a.m. on a Sunday morning, while waiting for him since 7 a.m. You may laugh, but nothing speaks any more than honoring people's time. I helped him set up the chairs, it was a new start-up church and I helped set up the sound system and did everything else he needed help with.

When we were finished I looked at him and said, "Pastor, if you will give me a key to this church, you never have to open it again and set up anything. You can go pray and I will take care of it." I didn't need a word from God to do that. I wasn't waiting for a vision or a dream from the Lord to offer help. I just saw his need and was willing to fill it.

Find a need and fill it! That's the only word you need. Today it seems to be the complete opposite. Many say you should take care of yourself first and then you can consider the church and its needs. I'm not saying that the church shouldn't help people, because that is what we are called to do. But the attitude of "me first" is not the attitude of an armorbearer.

Things have truly changed in today's culture, but it has not in Heaven's culture. My pastor gave me the key and never looked back. He didn't need to because I had it covered. Where are the armorbearers for the leaders today who will step up and take a key and help? Ten years passed after taking that key, and God spoke to me to write the *Armorbearer* book and release a revelation to that generation. I witnessed the hand of the Lord move on that book and it started with me taking the key from my pastor, just to help.

Now as a father, pastor, and a spiritual father, I'm asking how many people in the church and all the spiritual sons and daughters who will read this book desire a real impartation of the armorbearer spirit, the very Spirit of Jesus Himself. Don't look for me to lay hands on you; rather, get up and run to your pastor and ask for the key. Then don't ever let your pastor open the door again. Give honor to whom honor is due!

3. Armorbearers exhibit excellence.

> *Then this Daniel distinguished himself above the governors and satraps, because an **excellent spirit** was in him; and the king gave thought to setting him over the whole realm* (Daniel 6:3).

What is excellence?

- Natural talent and knowing your potential. An uncut diamond has a wealth of unrealized possibility and brilliance.

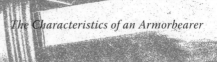

An uncut diamond has
a wealth of unrealized
possibility and
brilliance.

- Invest in yourself and believe in yourself. Daniel knew the gift he had and was not ashamed to use it. The gift led him into the lion's den, but also moved him into promotion. Not sure how fun that is, but if ministry were easy, everyone would do it.

- Integrity. When you have integrity, your word means everything.

- Passion. It speaks to all who are around you that you believe that God has called you to do something. The big "Yes" in you is discovered through your passion.

- Creativity and innovation. The Creator of the universe dwells in you! Never say you can't have a creative thought. Bring your gift to your church and help make a difference. We need what you have to offer.

- Commitment. It's time to bloom where God has planted you.

- Show up. Be there for someone else.

- Contribute. Give something, find something to give, or just give your time.

My twin brother, Dr. Jerry Nance, president of Teen Challenge International with 1,200 centers around the world, shared with me about his heart for excellence. He was staying one night at the Ritz Carlton hotel. When he pulled up to the front of the hotel, a young man opened his door and said, "Mr. Nance, we are glad to have you for the weekend." Jerry said thanks and then the bellhop came immediately out to get his luggage and said, "Mr. Nance, we will take care of everything for you, so go ahead to the check-in counter on the left, inside the door." He entered the hotel lobby and the clerk at the counter, before he could say anything, said, "Mr. Nance, how are you?"

How did they know what he looked like and how did they put his face to his name? Can you imagine the homework behind that? Someone did some serious checking. And how excellent it was for him to hear his name called when he first arrived. Vince Lombardi said, "Perfection is not attainable, but if we chase perfection we can catch excellence." That's a mouth full. If you don't go for excellence then you will settle for mediocrity.

The following is a portion of a survey done by the Ritz Carlton in transforming a dissatisfied customer into a satisfied customer. In this survey they found the customer wanted three things:

1. The product delivered with excellence. Clean sheets and a clean room.

2. The product delivered in a timely manner. They didn't want to have to wait when they arrived.

3. The product delivered with friendliness and kindness, the most important of all.

That's not really asking much. It is really about attitude. Armorbearers will take care of the church because they can see it as God's House and not just a building. They do everything the best they can because they value the church the same way Jesus loves the church.

> *Then this **Daniel distinguished himself** above the governors and satraps, because an **excellent spirit was in him**; and the king gave thought to setting him over the whole realm* (Daniel 6:3).

An armorbearer has a heart and attitude to do whatever the task is with excellence. Booker T. Washington said, *"Excellence is to do a common thing in an uncommon way."*

A great New Testament example of an armorbearer with an excellent spirit in a local church is Epaphras: *"As you also learned from Epaphras, our dear fellow servant, who is a faithful minister of Christ on your behalf, who also declared to us your love in the Spirit"* (Colossians 1:7-8). Here we see Epaphras was a true armorbearer to Paul. He carried a servant's heart connected to the love that Paul had for the church at Colossae.

He truly represented Paul's heart of passion for the church. He was also said to be a faithful minister to the church. He was there for the purpose of caring for the flock of Colossae. Paul had full confidence that armorbearer Epaphras was there to pray and minister to the church in the good times and hard times. He was a proven minister on their behalf. Armorbearer Epaphras was an encourager to all the church at Colossae.

Paul also acknowledges armorbearer Epaphras' excellent heart of prayer: *"Epaphras, who is one of you, a bondservant of Christ, greets you, always laboring fervently for you in prayers, that you may stand perfect and complete in all the will of God"* (Colossians 4:12).

You say you are submitted, but you will never learn submission until you can submit when you disagree.

Wow! For Paul to have said that he must have been in intercession with Epaphras for Colossae and witnessed how his love and fervency for the church stood out during their prayer time.

Here is a man pouring out his heart before God for his church. That describes the spirit of excellence a pastor is looking for in his armorbearer: a servant's heart, faithful in duty, and a committed intercessor for the church.

— 9 —

LET'S ALL JUST
SUBMIT—LOL!

T erry Wayne Nance, you are the most stubborn kid on this planet. I am going to beat you within an inch of your life if you don't do what I told you to do," thus said Tommy Nance. My response was, "Dad, it's not fair or right for me to be held accountable for something my wonderful twin brother Jerry did—not me." Jerry was my wombmate for nine months.

Dad would always say, "You are getting punished because I know you had your hand in it and you are guilty by association." Be him right or be him wrong, it didn't matter to me because in my mind and my eyes it wasn't fair. I always responded to this kind of injustice and would tell Dad, "Be it right or be it wrong, in the eyes of Terry Nance and in the eyes of Almighty God, I am not going to do it. Hell itself will freeze over before I submit to something that I feel is unjust punishment. So proceed with the beating because I'm not moving!"

Now that was the way I was. It was not pretty for about five years with my dad. He wanted to oblige my request and attempted,

I felt, to end my precious life on this earth. He was going to beat that spirit out of me one way or the other. I was really fast when I was young, so he had to catch me first. If it were not for my wonderful mom, my time on earth would have been cut short.

I said all that to make the point that submission was not easy for me. I was not rebellious. It was only when I felt the Scripture being fulfilled that says parents should not provoke your children to wrath (Ephesians 6:4). That was my favorite Scripture growing up, but it was not always the case. I know I deserved most of it because I would think of something mischievous to do and Jerry would act it out—which gave me deniability.

When the Jesus Movement hit Arkansas in 1973, everything changed. I wanted to please Jesus so much that I decided to give honor to my dad by doing what he asked. It took all the meanness out of both of us, and we actually formed a pretty good relationship. But I still carry a very righteous anger when I see injustice. What the Lord did was teach me how to keep my mouth shut and flow with authority, even when I thought they were wrong.

The one truth we have to agree with is that the Bible is the final authority. If the Bible says to submit to authority, then I will stand before Jesus who is the Word made flesh and give account. For me that settled it. I determined to flow with authority and let God fight my battles. Boy, did peace and promotion come through it!

Look at the story of Hagar. You talk about injustice. She was done wrong by Abraham and Sarah:

So he went in to Hagar, and she conceived. And when she saw that she had conceived, her mistress became despised in her eyes. Then Sarai said to Abram, "My wrong be upon you! I gave my maid into your embrace; and when she saw that she had conceived, I became despised in her eyes. The Lord judge between you and me." So Abram said to Sarai, "Indeed your maid is in your hand; do to her as you please." And when Sarai dealt harshly with her, she fled from her presence (Genesis 16:4-6).

Now whose fault was this? Sure wasn't Hagar's. She was the first real victim in the Bible. I feel God should have taken Abraham and Sarah to the woodshed for this one; but I am not God. Now listen to what the Lord says, revealing part of His nature to Hagar:

*Now the Angel of the Lord found her by a spring of water in the wilderness, by the spring on the way to Shur. And He said, "Hagar, Sarai's maid, where have you come from, and where are you going?" She said, "I am fleeing from the presence of my mistress Sarai." The Angel of the Lord said to her, "**Return** to your mistress, **and submit** yourself under her hand." Then the Angel of the Lord said to her, "I will multiply your descendants exceedingly, so that they shall not be counted for multitude." And the Angel of the Lord said to her: "Behold, you are with child, and you shall bear a son. You shall call his* *name Ishmael, Because the Lord has heard your afflic-tion. He shall be a wild man; His hand shall be against every man, And every man's hand against him. And he shall dwell in the presence of all his brethren." Then she called the name of the Lord who spoke to her, You-Are-the-God-Who-Sees; for she said, "Have I also here seen Him who sees me?"* (Genesis 16:7-13).

"Return and submit because I have a plan for you and the boy." That is hard to swallow until God reveals that His nature is I Am The God Who Sees. I am not saying stay in an abusive relation-ship in a church. When Saul picked up a spear and threw it at David, it was time to leave. David didn't need a word from God. But most the time ours is a problem we have with authority that needs to come under God's hand and God's Kingdom.

Philippians 2:5 says, *"Let this mind be in you which was also in Christ Jesus."* So that settles it. I am to have the attitude of Jesus who humbled Himself, submitted Himself, and was obedient unto death for us. He set the example of submission to the will of His Father. Authority will never cease. We will still have to submit even in the millennial reign of Christ.

And it shall come to pass that everyone who is left of all the nations which came against Jerusalem shall go up from year to year to worship the King, the Lord of hosts, and to keep the Feast of Tabernacles. And it shall be that whichever of the families of the earth do not come

The one truth we have to agree with is that the Bible is the final authority.

up to Jerusalem to worship the King, the Lord of hosts,
on them there will be no rain (Zechariah 14:16-17).

If the nations do not submit to worship Jesus when He is here on this planet reigning as King, the Bible is clear, if you don't worship you will not get rain. So authority is not going anywhere. We have to learn this so we can become armorbearer servants like Jesus. The revelation that helped me was this—*authority is not on the person, but on the office.* All authority comes from God.

Let every soul be subject to the governing authorities.
For there is no authority except from God, and the
authorities that exist are appointed by God. Therefore
whoever resists the authority resists the ordinance of
God, and those who resist will bring judgment on them-
selves (Romans 13:1-2).

The Bible says there is no authority except from God. I'll make this very clear. I am not talking about unconditional submission. If anyone who commands you to do something that violates the Scripture, you have a higher authority to which you must submit. I have seen this happen, but not very often. In the local church, submission to authority begins with just checking your kids into the nursery. There are times when parents need to abide by the rules. It's really not that big of a deal. My youngest daughter, McKenna, who is a Generation Z, will argue with a stop sign. I love her spirit, but she has had to learn a lesson in her local church. That's just the way we do it around here! On every level in our life, it is wise to learn how to flow with the way things are done in certain environments, as in local churches. Just settle down and do what Jesus would do, submit!

Let's look at these Scriptures:

> *I urge you, brethren—you know the household of Stephanas, that it is the first fruits of Achaia, and that they have devoted themselves to the ministry of the saints— that you also **submit** to such, and to everyone who works and labors with us* (1 Corinthians 16:15-16).

> *Submitting to one another in the fear of God* (Ephesians 5:21).

> ***Obey** those who rule over you, and be submissive, for they watch out for your souls, as those who must give account. Let them do so with joy and not with grief, for that would be unprofitable for you* (Hebrews 13:17).

> *Therefore **submit** yourselves to every ordinance of man for the Lord's sake, whether to the king.... Servants, **be submissive** to your masters with all fear, not only to the good and gentle, but also to the harsh* (1 Peter 2:13,18).

The word *submit* in the Greek means "to subordinate; to be under obedience, put under, subdue unto, to be in subjection, submit yourself unto, to submit to one's control, to yield to one's admonition or advice, to obey, be subject to." It is very clear that

God says we are to submit and flow with leaders in the church and the workplace. We are here to set the example of how Jesus would live today. The authority is on the office. I submit to the office whether or not I like the one in the office.

Think about it, Peter, James, John, the apostle Paul, and all the disciples submitted under the authority of the lunatic Nero who was emperor of Rome. Most of them died under his reign. They taught us to pray and submit so that it would a witness of Jesus. They didn't submit when it violated Jesus' command, but Jesus told them to submit to authority. So it's the office you submit to.

When I left after twenty-three years in a ministry, I gave up my keys, parking spot, every perk and title because I was no longer in authority. By the way, they also stopped paying me a salary. That's on me because I resigned from the office. Authority follows offices, not people.

Why is this spirit of armorbearer, servanthood, and submission so important in the church?

- It makes someone else's needs your priority
- It lifts up others
- It moves contemplation into action
- It gives honor to the men and women of God
- It goes and gets the donkey for the Master
- It prepares the people to sit down and eat
- It takes the load off the spiritual leader
- It moves you to pray for your leaders
- It joins the leaders in caring for the church

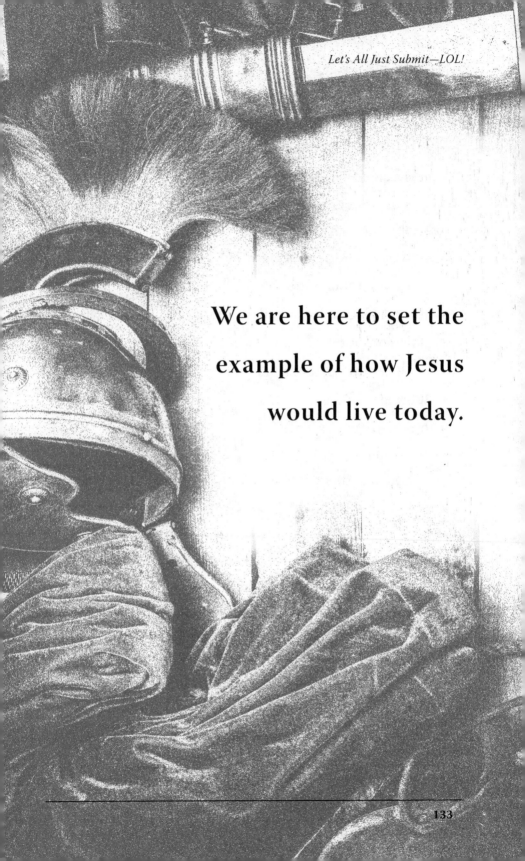

We are here to set the example of how Jesus would live today.

- It helps you to stop thinking of yourself
- It is always there to help
- It is a commitment to God and others
- It is a spirit of protection for the church and the men and women of God
- It lives in the armor of God ready for warfare
- It is the spirit of leadership
- It is the biggest threat to the present culture of the world
- It demonstrates love
- It carries the heart of a military officer
- It brings in a sense of security
- It represents Heaven on earth
- It is a spirit under submission to God and those He has placed in authority
- It is someone who can be trusted

The armorbearer servant leadership is the culture of Heaven. We are in a fight today over culture. Either the corrupt ways of humankind will win or the ways of the Kingdom will possess this earth. God did not call the church to sit around and wait till Jesus comes and gets us off this planet. Our Father is trying His best to get on this planet and bring all into His saving grace.

A culture is a way of life of a group of people—behaviors, beliefs, values, and symbols that they accept, generally without thinking about them, and are passed along by communication and imitation from one generation to the next. Culture is symbolic communication.

Now wait just a minute and let's together think about what would happen if just in the Church alone a spirit of armorbearing was released into our culture. Wow! The love of serving and submitting to one another would explode in our churches. We would be more concerned for each other than for ourselves. Can you imagine a pastor walking in and people have already taken care of everything for him. He would never have to think about how to get something done. The church team would be flowing in a harvest mindset and ready to reach the world.

The armorbearer spirit becomes something that is not just taught, it is something we become. You can't create your culture until you discover and determine your values.

In an armorbearer culture we choose to value each other, submit to authority, and run with the vision of God's house. We take these values we desire in our lives and church and emulate those values everywhere we go. The world sees a united Church, feels the power of a submitted Church, and will experience the glory of the glorified Church.

We therefore bring Heaven's culture to earth.

— 10 —

THE SIDELINE CHURCH— GOD'S SECRET ARMY

I dedicate this chapter to all the believers who have not discovered their assignment from God yet, and to all the prodigals who have walked away from theirs. The Spirit of God is passionately reaching for you. His love is not based on what you can do for Him but what He has already done for you. We are the focus of His love.

> *How blessed is God! And what a blessing he is! He's the Father of our Master, Jesus Christ, and takes us to the high places of blessing in him. Long before he laid down earth's foundations, he had us in mind, had settled on us as the focus of his love, to be made whole and holy by his love. Long, long ago he decided to adopt us into his family through Jesus Christ. (What pleasure he took in planning this!) He wanted us to enter into the celebration of his lavish gift-giving by the hand of his beloved Son* (Ephesians 1:3-6 The Message).

That is one of the most encouraging passages of Scriptures. He has chosen us as the focus of His love. Now that is grace! But remember John 1:17, *"For the law was given through Moses, but grace and truth came through Jesus Christ."*

Ephesians 2:7-10 in The Message Bible tells us:

> *Now God has us where he wants us, with all the time in this world and the next to shower grace and kindness upon us in Christ Jesus. Saving is all his idea, and all his work. All we do is trust him enough to let him do it. It's God's gift from start to finish! We don't play the major role. If we did, we'd probably go around bragging that we'd done the whole thing! No, we neither make nor save ourselves. God does both the making and saving. He creates each of us by Christ Jesus to join him in the work he does, the good work he has gotten ready for us to do, work we had better be doing.*

We are passionately loved by our Father—grace; called to join in His work—truth. There are two sides to the Kingdom coin. I have never met anyone who enjoyed standing on the sideline during a football game. You know you have potential, but the opportunity to prove it has not been given. For the believer, you are called to join Jesus in His work and the giftings and potential is in you—you just haven't awakened yet to it. God's Spirit is moving to get us into the harvest game in which God has committed Himself.

Now there is no way the whole Body of Christ can step up and be part of the ministry of helps or the inner circle of armorbearers.

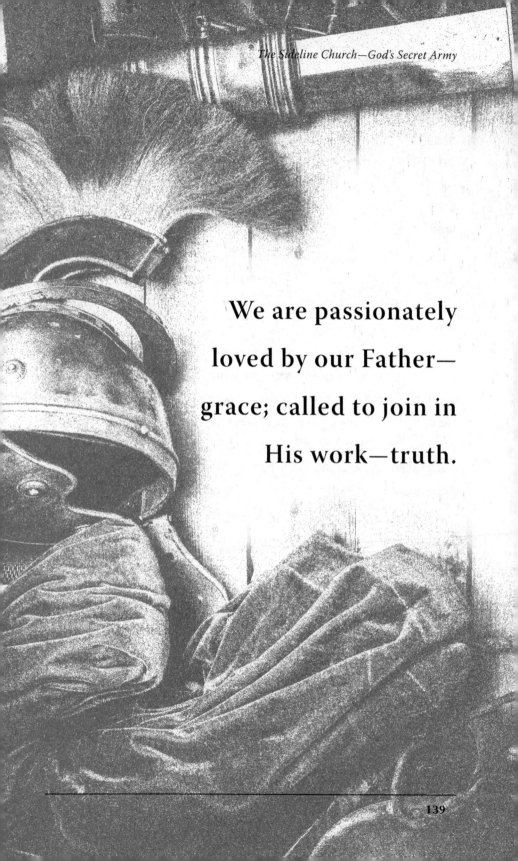

We are passionately loved by our Father—grace; called to join in His work—truth.

So what are you supposed to do? You are called to influence people for Jesus in the marketplace and raise up disciple makers everywhere you go. And the only way you will do it is by taking on the spirit of an armorbearer. The anointing that Jesus Himself operated in by coming to earth to serve humanity is the same way you will do it.

Back to Ephesians: *"Therefore be imitators of God as dear children. And walk in love, as Christ also has loved us and given Himself for us, an offering and a sacrifice to God for a sweet-smelling aroma"* (Ephesians 5:1-2).

God is not suggesting that we think of ourselves as little gods, but He is commanding us to take on His nature and represent Him in the marketplace. Of the 98 percent of all Christians in the marketplace, only 2 percent represent inner-circle armorbearers or pastors and other spiritual leaders. Marketplace ministry is defined as evangelism or other Christian activities that are targeted toward the secular workplace, a calling to influence.

It is to our discredit that some Christian leaders leave the impression that the Kingdom of God totally revolves around them. I heard an individual teach and declare that God only speaks through the mouth of His prophets—if that is true, we are all in trouble. That false teaching creates a spirit of elitism.

According to John 16:13, we *all* can hear the voice of God. Those of us called to lead the Body of Christ in the sacred area need to remember we are no more special than those God called to the secular world, the workplace ministry. Again, 2 percent of believers work in the sacred, and 98 percent in the secular. So as pastors, you tell me who we need to focus on.

Look at this Scripture:

> *Now Saul was consenting to his death. At that time a*
> *great persecution arose against the church which was*
> *at Jerusalem; and they were all scattered throughout*
> *the regions of Judea and Samaria, except the apostles.*
> *...Therefore those who were scattered went everywhere*
> *preaching the word* (Acts 8:1,4).

How have we missed this? The apostles during the persecution stayed in Jerusalem but the Church was *scattered everywhere preaching the word.* Who were scattered? The apostles or the Church? The Church! If you are a Christian standing on the sideline, if you turn around and look at all the people in the stands, you will find who you're really called to help. The Church in these Scriptures is revealed in two different functions—the gathered Church and the scattered Church.

The apostles stayed at home while the Church was released to take Jesus to the marketplace where all the people are. The word *preach* means to go model Jesus to those in your sphere of influence, to win as many as you can and bring them into the local church to be fed and discipled.

Pastors, your true inner-circle armorbearers may be found in the marketplace and not in the seminary. Over a year ago I walked into Hideaway Pizza with two of my elders and we sat down to order. A young lady with some cool tattoos came up to wait on us. We ordered our food but in the middle of it we all began to share the love of Jesus with her. It wasn't busy that night, so she was able to visit for a while. Then one of my elders ministered a prophetic word to her and she broke and began to share her story. She had been in Teen Challenge and had struggled in some areas of her life. We just loved her and encouraged her in her walk with Jesus.

Finally one of my elders asked her if she had ever read the *Armorbearer,* because the book is used in most Teen Challenge curricula. She said, "Of course," and was reading though it right then. He laughed and said, "Well, would you like to meet the author?" The look on her face was worth a million dollars. We all knew God had set up a divine appointment for her. I invited her to church since she had no church home, and the next Wednesday there she was and she has never left. She is now my youth pastor and I can proudly say a spiritual daughter to Kim and me.

Jesus said to His disciples in Matthew 9:37-38, *"The harvest truly is plentiful, but the laborers are few. Therefore pray the Lord of the harvest to send out laborers into His harvest."* Jesus didn't ask the disciples to pray for the harvest, He asked them to pray for laborers to be sent out. You are the laborer He is praying for. God always answers Jesus' prayers.

I agree with Jesus that an anointing is falling on the sideline church to thrust you into the harvest of the marketplace so you can preach the gospel everywhere you go. Don't scream, "I'm not a preacher!" Because you are. You have the Holy Spirit in you and Jesus needs you to join in the work. Grace is the empowerment to walk in truth. You are a harvest hand called to be a harvester. Preaching is simply proclaiming the good news about Jesus. When I tell a waiter that Jesus loves him deeply and wants a relationship with him, I have just preached. So all believers are called to preach.

> *For the love of Christ compels us, because we judge thus: that if One died for all, then all died.... Now all things are of God, who has reconciled us to Himself through Jesus Christ, and* **has given us the ministry of reconciliation**, *that is, that God was in Christ reconciling the world to Himself, not imputing their trespasses to them, and has committed to us the word of reconciliation. Now then,* **we are ambassadors for Christ**, *as though God were pleading through us: we implore you on Christ's behalf, be reconciled to God* (2 Corinthians 5:14, 18-20).

These Scripture verses are here to awaken the sideline armor-bearer church, to compel us to love people like Jesus. Compel means I become a prisoner of His love. I can't help but share it because my Daddy God has His big arms around me and is squeezing love out of me for you.

As a marketplace armorbearer, I have my ministry to: Go reconcile the world to Jesus. Go get the lost people, win them to Jesus, and train them to become armorbearer disciple makers. I talk about being a disciple maker in the next chapter.

One of the most powerful Scriptures to me about destiny is found in Second Timothy 1:9: *"who has* **saved us and called us** *with a holy calling, not according to our works, but* **according to**.

His own purpose and grace which was *given to us in Christ Jesus before time began."*

Here it is: *You are called! You have a purpose! You have received grace! And it all happened before time began!* Now just try sleeping on that Scripture—your mind will go crazy over it. The fact is, He's God and before He said, "Let there be light!" He knew who you were, called you, put an assignment in you for you to accomplish, and gave His grace to fulfill it. Wow! The anointing to write this book was in me before I was ever born. I was His thought before I became my mother's son. Now I must line up with His thoughts for me and be obedient to Him. All my identity is found in Him and not in my upbringing.

You may not understand your giftings right now, but you can help your pastor by being a marketplace evangelist and influence your coworkers toward Jesus.

Now I want to address all the prodigals reading this chapter. You are not really sure how on earth you got the book and how you got to this chapter. Well, you're here by the divine calling of God and His ever-reaching love for you.

I know you say no one has a clue where you are and what's going on in your life—and the truth is, you're right. I don't like it either when people insinuate that they feel my pain. No one feels your pain but you. They may identify with it because of a similar thing they have walked through, but they are not you.

The prodigal in Luke 15 was called a son of the house, not a servant. That means he lived with all the privileges of a son. Sons have favor that others do not. When my twin brother and I came home from college to my parents' home, we always said, "Hello Mom,

Dad, we're glad to be here. Can we have the key to the shoe store?" My parents owned the Shoe Box in Magnolia, Arkansas. Jerry and I went to the store, locked the door behind us and got what we called the five-finger discount. That means our shoes were free at our dad's expense. We never wore cheap shoes, only the best. Never settled for just one pair either. Now you say, "Brother Terry, why would you do that?" Simple, I am a son of the Nance household with privileges of a son that I didn't mind enjoying.

The prodigal was a son of the house and for some reason unknown, he wanted his inheritance and left. Could be that he thought the inheritance was only for the older brother or someone maybe was influencing him to leave. Of that, we are not sure; nevertheless, he left. After wasting all he was given, without any hope of restoration, he was broke and living with the swine of the world's culture without a friend to his name. With everything gone, it's either suicide or eat with the pigs.

Satan is lord over the swine of the world's culture. You end up hung, snared, lost, and forgotten. I know this is touching someone. God is reaching His grace and love to you now. You may not want hear this, but the truth is Jesus hurts more than you will ever hurt. He experienced separation from His Father so He could take your rejection and restore your identity as an heir. You are a son or daughter of His House—yet you are eating from the swine of the world's culture. You're lost in your hurt and pain.

There is no way out except by coming to yourself—realizing where you are. No one can pull you out until you say "Enough!" The prodigal came to himself and knew at least the servants at home had clean sheets and decent meals, so he headed for home.

Enough was enough! The thought of being rejected by his father was real. He didn't deserve anything but he also knew that his father was merciful. With that thought he knew he could fall on his dad's mercy.

We serve a merciful God who loves us in the middle of our junk and continually reaches out to us, ready to receive us back into His arms. Satan cannot stop you from heading home. He can influence, but he can't stop you. The story demonstrates God's love and restoration. When the father saw the son, he ran to him. Your Father God always celebrates any movement toward Him. Just like the prodigal son and father in the Bible story, God wants to grab you, embrace you, and weep for joy that you have returned to Him.

When the son responds with a broken heart of repentance and says, "Let me live as a servant and not a son," the fiery compassion of the father screams, "I will not hear of it!" He tells his servants, "Bring my best robe, sandals, and kill my best cow. We are having steak tonight! My son who was lost has now returned and I am now complete forever." (See Luke 15:11-32.)

When you return to your calling there will be celebration, not toleration. It's time to get up and head back to the family of God. Your leaders love you and are ready to help in the restoration process. The local church will always be dysfunctional because the people are mostly believers, not disciples. They are in the process of becoming, and by grace they will become.

But you are called to bring your function to this dysfunction and help get it under God's control and into His Kingdom. Let's pray together:

We serve a merciful
God who loves us
in the middle
of our junk.

"Father, we love you. You have called us and given us assignments to fulfill on this earth. Please forgive me for the hurt and pain I feel toward my pastor and the Church. I know I am a child of the King and a member of Your House. I ask for your grace to come now as I begin my way back home."

— 11 —

INTENTIONAL RELATIONAL ARMORBEARER DISCIPLESHIP

I ntentional relational armorbearer discipleship—wow, that's a mouthful! But every word carries a powerful message that when combined moves us into the message of Jesus for these last days. I dedicate this chapter to all the pastors and spiritual leaders who are struggling with this current culture. We all have to make real changes to reach this next generation. When it comes to leadership style, you are either positional or relational. You can dice and slice it all kinds of ways, but honestly there are only two categories—positional or relational.

When we study Jesus, we discover He was a relational leader. Of course He knew His title and position, but He never moved the people by His title. It was always relational. Let's go back and remember the things the armorbearer desires from us as leaders:

1. I want you to know that I can handle your human side and not lose respect.

2. I want you to know I truly desire to be your Timothy in the same way Timothy was to Paul, a true son in the faith.

3. I want you to know I would love to have some hang time with you. I promise no familiarity.

4. I want you to know I desire relationship.

These points came from the group of Millennials I met with. They are after spiritual relationship and some good old hang time.

Kim and I have made it a mandate to spend quality time with them because we now see clearly they are our future. We recently met with twenty of them and gave them permission to ask any question they wanted. They wrote them down and shared their hearts. Their questions were awesome. I will go back in a week or so after writing this manuscript and answer the questions in another hang time meeting with them. It's going to be fun. Kim and I are not holding anything back. That's relational.

Positional wants respect and honor with no investment, and that just won't happen anymore. We must be willing to make this change.

Intentional means "deliberate, calculated, conscious, done on purpose, intended, planned, meant, considered, studied, knowing, willful, wanton, purposeful, purposive, purposed, premeditated, preplanned, thought out in advance, prearranged." You can

Jesus was intentional
when He was ready to
choose His disciples.

clearly see being intentional carries weight in choosing. Jesus was intentional when He was ready to choose His disciples:

> *Now it came to pass in those days that* **He went out to the mountain to pray, and continued all night in prayer to God.** *And when it was day, He called His disciples to Himself; and from them He chose twelve whom He also named apostles* (Luke 6:12-13).

Jesus prayed and depended on the Holy Spirit to select the right ones. Jesus spent all night in prayer before choosing. We make mistakes by choosing the most qualified, while God sometimes chooses the least qualified. That is not always the case but the Holy Spirit always knows what is in our hearts. We have to get in prayer before selecting our team. The Holy Spirit selected this bunch of everyday guys and turned them into models of Jesus. He picked them out with intention and it became His responsibility to journey with them and build a relationship. This required them being open to His love, His questioning of their faith, involving them in ministry, celebrating their success, and challenging their mistakes and their unbelief. Jesus' approach was intentional, relational, servanthood (armorbearer) disciples. I think you get the picture here.

The church today has become a group of believers with few disciples. This is the reason ministry becomes difficult, because we have not taken the time to train up armorbearer disciples. I believe what you have learned in this book will help you develop your team. Discipleship is the missing ingredient in the church today.

Jesus says in John 17:4, *"I have glorified You on the earth. I have finished the work which You have given Me to do."* Now let's examine this statement Jesus made. He said He had finished the work the Father had sent Him to do. He hadn't gone to the Cross yet, so what is He referring to? The work was His disciples. Listen to the rest of His prayer:

> *I have manifested Your name to the men whom You have given Me out of the world. They were Yours, You gave them to Me, and they have kept Your word. Now they have known that all things which You have given Me are from You. For I have given to them the words which You have given Me; and they have received them, and have known surely that I came forth from You; and they have believed that You sent Me. I pray for them. I do not pray for the world but for those whom You have given Me, for they are Yours. ...As You sent Me into the world, I also have sent them into the world* (John 17:6-9, 18).

The work Jesus finished was His discipleship. He had fathered the disciples, loved them, rebuked them, and now was ready to die for them, knowing only John would go all the way with Him to the Cross. He knew after the empowerment of the Holy Spirit these eleven men would change the world. His intentional relational discipleship paid off. These guys carried His armorbearer servant heart, and they would change the world.

Pastors, leaders, and ministry will not work the way it used to work. We used to simply hand out the *Armorbearer* book and tell them do their calling exactly this way because this is the way it is. Today they will hand it back and say, "Not until I know you as a spiritual father am I going to do it."

Now don't fight this reality! This is the Holy Spirit building His family team that will impact this world. Look closely at how Jesus built an intentional relational team. Jesus was intentional:

- He went after the ones the Holy Spirit directed Him to choose.
- Jesus prayed all night before choosing.
- He called His disciples to Himself. Those God chooses to be your armorbearers will have to be called to you.
- These disciples became apostles through servanthood. They carried His spirit inside themselves. Your true team will always carry your spirit.
- He turned these believers into armorbearer disciples.
- The church is full of believers, not disciples. Jesus knew it takes time to develop disciples, you need to have the same wisdom.
- Disciple makers was His ultimate goal.
- He modeled it for them.
- He gave Himself to them.
- He exposed their weaknesses.

Discipleship is the

missing ingredient in

the Church today.

- He challenged their faith.

- He tested their love for one another.

- He showed them what success was.

- He allowed them to see His weakness.

- He let them see the lion side of His personality by driving out the money changers.

- He let them see His human side when He wept over Jerusalem.

- He let them see His anointing when ministering to the sick.

- He never condemned them.

- He delegated His gifts to them.

- He allowed them to take risks.

- He was always there to clean up their mess.

- He taught them Kingdom servanthood.

Jesus was their spiritual Father. He said, "To see me is to see the Father." He modeled it for us. You leave no legacy without spiritual sons and daughters. If you haven't done this yet, you have missed the Jesus model. One day in prayer the Holy Spirit directed me to Matthew 28: *"Go therefore and **make disciples** of all the nations, baptizing them in the name of the Father and of the Son and of the Holy Spirit, teaching them to observe all things that I have commanded you; and lo, I am with you always, even to the end of the age. Amen"* (Matthew 28:19-20).

We are called to make disciples, which is the call of every leader. The Lord witnessed to my heart and said, "Terry, when I said to go make disciples, I really meant *go make disciples.* When you stand before Me, I will open the book of rewards and see who the disciples you have made for Me are." This commission from Jesus is not the Great Suggestion!

So where have we missed it? We have focused on building cool places of worship and providing all the tools to make the believers happy, but the one thing many haven't done is make true disciples. A true armorbearer disciple is one who is following Jesus, committed to being changed by Jesus, and who will become a disciple maker, just as Jesus did. As leaders we need to say to our armorbearers, "Come follow me as I follow Christ." This is relationship. We change the world one disciple at a time.

Right now in my life I have four young men I meet with on a weekly basis. I use this time to listen and pour love and ministry into them. I've never had this done for me, but I decided to become the spiritual father I always wanted. Kim and I have committed our lives to this and we are witnessing a beautiful change in our Millennials and Generation Zs. Jesus modeled the Father in front of His disciples, and we are called to model Jesus as best we can in front of those around us. My time is my investment into their lives. What I have discovered is many do not have a father or mother who set a godly example for them in the home.

During these last days, God wants to use us all through intentional relational discipleship. Jim Putman has written some incredible books on the subject. His material will help you as it has helped me.

Let's look at the Bible's definition of the difference in the generational cultures on the earth at this time. Now people much smarter than I say we have the:

- The Greatest Generation, born between 1901-1924

- The Silent Generation, 1925-1945

- Baby Boomer Generation, 1946-1964

- Generation X, 1965-1980

- Millennials (Generation Y, GenNext), 1981-1996

- Generation Z or iGen, 1997-2012

- Generation Alpha, born after 2010

I will be the first to say I have learned a lot by studying the different generations. But can we find anything in the Bible that sets the generations apart and gives them names? Yes!

Look at the book of Acts:

> *And it shall come to pass in the last days, says God, that I will pour out of My Spirit on all flesh; your **sons and your daughters shall prophesy**, your **young men shall see visions**, your **old men shall dream** dreams. And on My menservants and on my maidservants I will pour out My Spirit in those days; and they shall prophesy. I will show wonders in heaven above and signs in the earth beneath: Blood and fire and vapor of smoke. The sun shall be turned into darkness, and the moon into*

blood, before the coming of the great and awesome day of the Lord" (Acts 2:17-20).

God distinctly separates generations; and I interpret this as God dividing cultures into three age categories:

- Prophetic, ages 3-24
- Vision, ages 25-54
- Dream, ages 55 and up

The children and students as the prophetic team must be empowered by God and taught that they have not received a baby Holy Spirit. They are prophetic as they proclaim God's goodness and speak the wisdom and righteousness of God into their generation. They have the voice of the Father for their peers. We are going to be amazed how God pours out His Spirit upon them to shake the schools and colleges around the United States and the world.

The visionaries must stay in prayer for new vision from God to reach His world. These are our wonderful Millennials and Zs. They prophesy to the young children and teach them the gifts that God has instilled in each one of them, while always giving honor to the dream team and serving as their armorbearers.

The dream team must raise up armorbearer disciples that look for the vision of God. The dreamers are called to keep dreaming in God, and teach that nothing is impossible with God. I am a dreamer. We dreamers must stop trying to secure our base through our own insecurity, rather than opening our lives to others for legacy. We are to build legacy through relationship while encouraging the vision team to have visions.

God is pouring out His Spirit on us and we need to find out which team we are in and get in line to help each other. We must respect and love what God is doing with the vision team. A young lady came to me who is an artist. She asked my permission to do something very unusual. She asked me and my elders to come to an elder's home to experience what the Lord was instructing her to do. She handed us all a sheet of art paper and asked us to pray and then draw what we saw.

Now I have never heard of such a thing, but it was interesting. The Lord spoke to me at the first of the year and said to expect the unusual. This was very unusual. The woman wanted us to draw, and then she would help us interpret what the Holy Spirit was saying to us. Funny because I am no artist at all. Stick horses and stick men are about as good as it gets. But suddenly after prayer, I saw mountains so I drew a range of snow-capped mountains. Then I saw a climbing team headed up to the peak. I was finished in two minutes and turned it in while everyone else took thirty minutes or more.

The Lord spoke to me, "The Mountain is where you are leading this church, and it's My mountain you are on. The success of the church depends on unity and oneness of vision. Climbers depend on each other to survive the climb."

I have focused my energy on building those kinds of relationships with my team. It was a word from God. At this time, we have opened the door to allow this young lady to minister this gift once or twice a month with groups of six. She totally submitted her gift to the elders for our blessing. Now God is using her to release incredible gifts into people. She is a beautiful young Millennial and spiritual daughter to me now. I am so proud of her for being bold enough to stand up and use a wonderful gift for our Body. This is what I am talking about.

As a dreamer, I must free the armorbearer visionaries to have visions. I am listening, they are honoring, and the Kingdom is advancing. As leaders we cannot speak down to the next generation.

At 17 years old with hair down to the middle of my back, I was told I was a sinner and that God would only hear me if I would cut my hair. Well, I wasn't cutting my hair for some religious spirit. So we all just said bye to the church and went to the streets. Thank God for a pastor who loved us and took us all in.

We cannot lose this generation. If we do, we have no one to blame but ourselves. This brings me to Chapter 12 and what God is doing on earth now. It's time for a Reformation!

— 12 —

MALACHI—THE NEXT REFORMATION

Behold, I will send you Elijah the prophet before the coming of the great and dreadful day of the Lord. And he will turn the hearts of the fathers to the children, and the hearts of the children to their fathers, lest I come and strike the earth with a curse (Malachi 4:5-6).

Reformation means making changes to something with the intention of setting it back on the right path. When capitalized, the Reformation refers specifically to the Protestant Reformation in Europe, which was a religious change instigated in 1517 by Protestants who wished to reform the Catholic Church. Church history records how the Catholic church at that time kept the written Word of God from the masses to keep them controlled through spiritual blindness.

Martin Luther came preaching that "The just shall live by faith" and the "Priesthood of the Believer." Those revelations are still reforming lives today all around the world. This happened 500 years ago. My question is this: When is the next Reformation? I truly believe it is the Malachi Reformation. The Bible plainly says before the Day of the Lord He will send the spirit of Elijah and He will turn the hearts of the fathers to the children and the children to the fathers.

The Lord said to me recently, "Terry, how can I be a Father to the fatherless unless I father though you?"

> *Sing to God, sing praises to His name; extol Him who rides on the clouds, by His name YAH, and rejoice before Him. A father of the fatherless, a defender of widows, is God in His holy habitation* (Psalm 68:4-5).

> *The poor and helpless ones trust in you, Lord, for you are famous for being the helper of the fatherless* (Psalm 10:14 TPT).

> *The orphans and the oppressed will be terrified no longer, for you will bring them justice, and no one will trouble them* (Psalm 10:18 TPT).

I am dedicating this chapter to all the sons and daughters in the Body of Christ who are crying out to God—not for instructors, but fathers. I also dedicate this chapter to the fathers and mothers who read this and the Spirit of the Lord quickens your heart for this fatherless generation. Malachi is not talking about just the fathers in the home because they will never understand

How can I be a Father

to the fatherless unless

I father though you?

what fathering is until they see spiritual fathering in the Church. This call is for all the pastors, leaders, and disciple makers being raised up in the Church.

The Reformation is this—armorbearers transforming into spiritual sons and daughters, and pastors and Christian leaders transforming into spiritual fathers and mothers!

These are the facts in our world today:

- 63% of youth suicides are from fatherless homes (US Dept. of Health/Census)

- 90% of all homeless and runaway children are from fatherless homes

- 85% of all children who show behavior disorders come from fatherless homes (CDC)

- 80% of rapists with anger problems come from fatherless homes (Justice & Behavior, Vol. 14, p. 403-26)

- 71% of all high school dropouts come from fatherless homes (National Principals Association Report)

These statistics come from an article in World Press titled "The Fatherless Generation."[1] This article reveals what happens in modern-day American homes. And according to the U.S. Census Bureau, more than 1 in 4 children live without a father in the home.[2] As Christians, let's look at how this affects the church. If the church does not step up to the plate, we will lose this generation and bring the curse of Malachi upon us.

Malachi 4:5-6 brings a blessing or a curse—and we make the choice. God promises to pour His Spirit on the Prophetic Team, ages 3-24; Vision Team, ages 25-54; and Dream Team, age 55-until death. We must receive from Heaven a new mantle to spiritually father and mother this generation. To all you beautiful, wise, and available Dream Teamers, join me in promoting the visionaries and stop talking about how you feel discarded by them. Psalm 103:4-5 says, *"Who redeems your life from destruction, who crowns you with lovingkindness and tender mercies, who satisfies your mouth with good things, so that your youth is renewed like the eagle's."*

All you Eagle Dreamers, stand up with me and let's pour our godly heritage into this generation. Paul says to Timothy, *"when I call to remembrance the genuine faith that is in you, which dwelt first in your grandmother, Lois, and your mother Eunice, and I am persuaded is in you also"* (2 Timothy 1:5).

What an incredible heritage Timothy had. But here is the reality, the majority of the Visionary Generation, which the world calls the Millennials, were not raised that way. I am telling you the gospel truth. At the present time we are losing this battle and satan is laughing while we leaders scramble over which title I should have so someone might recognize my gift. How about taking hold of being a father and let the other titles go. When God looks down from Heaven, He doesn't see titles—He sees hearts!

Please don't throw this book in the corner. God is trying to get this message into the current leadership in the Church. We are called to set the example. Take a look at how God started the whole thing in the first place. Look at His intent from the very beginning.

So God created man in His own image; in the image of God He created him; male and female He created them. Then God blessed them, and God said to them, "Be fruitful and multiply; fill the earth and subdue it; have dominion over the fish of the sea, over the birds of the air, and over every living thing that moves on the earth" (Genesis 1:27-28).

Let's examine this Scripture passage very closely. The intent of God was for us to be blessed and have a ton of babies, to fill the earth with children. We are to teach our kids all about Him and have them spread the garden to the four corners of the earth. He can't wait for the day that He gets to walk with them the same way He walked with us. The earth was to be dominated by the children of Adam and Eve. His plan has never changed.

This current earth is to be dominated by the children of God, and the moms and dads of the Kingdom of God are called to model God. We, the dream team, are to model what it is like to walk with God to the vision team, who in turn model to the young prophetic team how to hear the voice of their Father God. That is what I mean by a Malachi Reformation. It is us receiving this word for such a time as this and fulfilling our role to release the spirit of fatherhood in this world. The apostle Paul says it this way: *"For though you might have ten thousand instructors in Christ, yet you do not have many fathers; for in Christ Jesus I have begotten you through the gospel"* (1 Corinthians 4:15).

I grew up in the generation of ten thousand teachers but few fathers. I don't blame the leaders I grew up under because the majority of them were moving in the revelation they had. But the Spirit of Truth will always move the Church into Kingdom building, which is generational, not seasonal. It is not my calling to try to build a huge church, it is my calling to father this generation and raise up disciple makers who can in turn become disciple makers and eventually father and mother someone else.

There are hundreds, if not thousands, of books from secular authors on leadership. Some of the greatest are Christian authors. The principles taught are for the most part incredible leadership information that can absolutely help in growing a church. But the one thing that cannot be taught in a book by secular leaders is how to be a spiritual father.

The apostles only modeled Jesus in His fathering role and His disciplining role. I do not know how the apostles made it without the books we have today. They never knew the ten principles of being a good leader and the ten of being the worst. They only knew Jesus, modeled Him, stayed in the Spirit, and loved this world. Spiritual fathering is something caught by our spirit and taught by the Spirit.

Please understand, I'm not saying ignore the books written. Some of the books on leadership I have read, and am reading, have given me incredible instruction concerning leadership. But the Spirit is crying out for the fathers and mothers to reach into the hell of this present culture and pull God's children out. Ten principles of leadership will not get it done. It will help but it will not pull them from satan's reach. It's going to take the Holy Spirit and us taking hold of Malachi as a word from God.

Delivering a Child

Kim and I know what it means to deliver a child out from hell. We adopted our son Alex from a Romanian orphanage when he was ten years old. When he was born he was left in the hospital for two years, never held, cuddled, nurtured by the love of his mom and dad. At two years of age his dad and stepmom brought him into the home where he was abused until he was six years old. God had mercy on Alex by putting him into an orphanage. At eight years old he climbed on the roof of the orphanage and cried to God to please give him parents from America so he could know what it was like to have a home and a real mom and dad.

I can't go into the full story of the adoption because there are not enough pages to tell all the miracles that began through the prayer of an orphaned child. But Heaven and earth moved for Alex, and God heard his cry. As he grew in our home, there were challenges because of the abuse he endured as a baby. A psychologist who had done major studies about Romanian orphans explained to me about attachment disorder, which is what happens to a baby who is never held, nurtured, and loved by their mom and dad. In the front of our brain, as the doctor explained it to me, are connections with our feelings of affection that bring a wholeness to a child.

When a baby is not held, cuddled, and loved there are no connections, causing an attachment disorder. It was hard for Alex and hard on us to hear him say, "Can I go live with those people? I like

Our legacy is in our
spiritual children, not
a big ministry.

it better over there." He didn't know what he was saying because he had no understanding of a real family. Not his fault.

Now look at what has happened in the Body of Christ. There is a spiritual attachment disorder because of the lack of fathers and mothers. The Millennials are running to other places rather than the family of God and the Church, just because they like it better over there. They have never felt the love of God and acceptance in their home and don't know what it is in the Church. To say, "Jesus loves you" is foreign to them. They are simply living off feelings and emotions because of the disorder in their lives. If we as the Dream Team do not rise up and bring them into our homes, we will lose them to the world's culture. All the toys in the world will not lure them into the Kingdom of God. Only God's love and His presence is going to reach them and bring them into their purpose.

Malachi is prophesying to us all—"I am going to turn the hearts of the fathers to the children." The spirit of Malachi is fathers and mothers claiming God's children right out of the hell of this culture and giving them their true identity and value. We are going to have to lay claim to our spiritual sons and daughters.

Laying Claim

Now I grew up in the "Name it and Claim it" movement era. I'm not criticizing this move. It taught me how to believe God in many areas of my life. But the reason you don't hear much about the movement today is because it never reached into the true heart of our Father, which is claiming the next generation for Him. It is us going after this generation with the same faith and tenacity we went after Alex.

My wife, Kim, was recently teaching at a women's encounter and in her teaching she made reference to a spiritual daughter of ours and said to everyone, "Terry and I have claimed her as ours. She belongs to us." That statement so touched a young lady's heart that she wept and wept over it. Her natural parents have not given her the identity they should have, therefore God is imparting it from her spiritual parents. I have heard it said many times that this is an orphan generation. What does that really mean? It means we will not get our identity from this world. We will only get it from God.

The problem I see is that the world has no clue what the heck we are talking about when we refer to an orphan generation. They live in a culture that tells them to fend for themselves and don't trust anyone. It is true that there is an orphan spirit among our youth. But we must realize their identity will only come to them when we are willing to be the humanity of the Father to the fatherless. We must take up the mantle of spiritual fatherhood. They have to see and experience God through us. We have to lead them to Jesus and father or mother them on their journey.

Being Claimed

What does the Bible say about being claimed?

> *Through our union with Christ **we too have been claimed by God as his own inheritance**. Before we were even born, he gave us our destiny; **that we would fulfill the plan of God who always accomplishes every purpose and plan in his heart*** (Ephesians 1:11 TPT).

Being claimed as a spiritual son or daughter releases inheritance and our destiny:

> *Timothy, you are my true spiritual son in the faith* (1 Timothy 1:2 TPT).

Being claimed over and over by Paul releases the impartation of Paul's spirit into Timothy:

> *My beloved son, I pray for a greater release of God's grace, love, and total well-being to flow into your life from God our Father and from our Lord Jesus Christ!* (2 Timothy 1:2 TPT)

Timothy is called a true son and a beloved son. This claiming sealed into him the power to represent Paul everywhere he went. What had been given from Timothy's mother and grandmother was released though Paul, claiming his sonship.

*Even though I have enough boldness in Christ that I could command you to do what is proper, I'd much rather make an appeal because of our friendship. So here I am, an old man, a prisoner for Christ, making my loving appeal to you. It is on behalf of my child, whose **spiritual father** I became while here in prison; that is, Onesimus. ...Formerly he was not useful or valuable to you, but now he is valuable to both of us. He is my very heart, and I've sent him back to you with this letter. I would have preferred to keep him at my side so that he could take your place as my helper during my imprisonment for the sake of the gospel. However, I did not want to make this decision without your consent, so that your act of kindness would not be a matter of obligation but out of willingness* (Philemon 1:8-9,11-14 TPT).

Spiritual fathering places a claim of protection over the son or daughter. It validates them to others.

Fully embrace God's correction as part of your training, for he is doing what any loving father does for his children. For who has ever heard of a child who never had to be corrected? We all should welcome God's discipline as the validation of authentic sonship. For if we have never once endured his correction it only proves we are strangers and not sons. And isn't it true that we respect our earthly fathers even though they corrected and disciplined us? Then we should demonstrate an even greater *respect for **God, our spiritual Father**, as we submit to his life-giving discipline. Our parents corrected us for the short time of our childhood as it seemed good to them. But God corrects us throughout our lives for our own good, giving us an invitation to share his holiness. Now all discipline seems to be more pain than pleasure at the time, yet later it will produce a transformation of character, bringing a harvest of righteousness and peace to those who yield to it* (Hebrews 12:7-11 TPT).

Spiritual fathers and mothers are able to discipline and bring correction. One of our spiritual daughters sent me this text:

> Do you remember when you sat me down on the couch a few years ago and talked to me about my passions and what I wanted to do with my life, you had a real hard talk with me about life? As hard as that talk was, it added value to my life, it showed me that you wanted to see me succeed and that you loved me. If you didn't have that conversation with me, no one would have. And now look, two years, maybe three, I have an amazing job and I am following God like never before. That wasn't easy, but meant a lot to me. I sure love you and Pastor Kim.

First Timothy 1:18 (TPT) says, *"Timothy, my son, I am entrusting you with this responsibility, in keeping with the very first prophecies that were spoken over your life, and are now in the process of fulfillment in this great work of ministry, in keeping with the prophecies spoken over you."*

Claiming a spiritual son or daughter releases their gifts. The Old Testament example is David finding Mephibosheth, Jonathan's son:

> *Now David said, "Is there still anyone who is left of the house of Saul, that I may show him kindness for Jonathan's sake?" ...Then the king said, "Is there not still someone of the house of Saul, to whom I may show the kindness of God?" ...And Ziba said to the king, "There is still a son of Jonathan who is lame in his feet." Then King David sent and brought him out of the house of Machir the son of Ammiel, from Lo Debar. Now when Mephibosheth the son of Jonathan, the son of Saul, had come to David, he fell on his face and prostrated himself. Then David said, "Mephibosheth?" And he answered, "Here is your servant!"*
>
> *So David said to him, "Do not fear, for I will surely show you kindness for Jonathan your father's sake, and will restore to you all the land of Saul your grandfather; and you shall eat bread at my table continually." Then he bowed himself, and said, "What is your servant, that you should look upon such a dead dog as I?" And the*

king called to Ziba, Saul's servant, and said to him, "I have given to your master's son all that belonged to Saul and to all his house. You therefore, and your sons and your servants, shall work the land for him, and you shall bring in the harvest, that your master's son may have food to eat. But Mephibosheth your master's son shall eat bread at my table always." Now Ziba had fifteen sons and twenty servants. Then Ziba said to the king, "According to all that my lord the king has commanded his servant, so will your servant do." "As for Mephibosheth," said the king, "he shall eat at my table like one of the king's sons" (2 Samuel 9:1, 3, 5-11).

Here is the truth of that for our generation. There are broken-covenant prodigals who left the church in fear and hurt. They now have no memory of the goodness of God and His love. But God is reminding His fathers and mothers, His disciple makers, His armorbearers, who are God's kings and queens to go get His broken family who no longer know their identity in Him and have been eating from the table of this demonic culture. God is saying, "Bring them to My table and let them eat from My presence. I am bringing them back and commanding you to go get them." That is a word from the Lord for you. We are going to have to say to them, "Please forgive me!"

Spiritual fathering and mothering begins with the heart of a servant armorbearer. You are fulfilling the great commission of Jesus to make disciple makers who are the real sons and daughters of God.

Bring them to My table and let them eat from My presence.

I leave you with Ephesians 5:1-2: *"Therefore be imitators* [models] *of God as dear children. And walk in love, as Christ also has loved us and given Himself for us, an offering and a sacrifice to God for a sweet-smelling aroma."*

The aroma of God will bring the Millennials running. That aroma may be the smell of some good free pizza at your house just to say, "I love you. I'm for you, and I'm here to journey with you." Suddenly spiritual fathers, mothers, and children are brought together by the love of Jesus—and *Malachi smiles!*

Endnotes

1. https://thefatherlessgeneration.wordpress.com/statistics; accessed May 6, 2020.

2. https://www.fatherhood.org/fatherhood-data-statistics; accessed May 6, 2020.

WAYS I CAN BE GOD'S ARMORBEARER

_____

_____

_____

_____

_____

_____

_____

_____

_____

_____

_____

_____

_____

_____

_____

_____

_____

_____

ABOUT THE AUTHOR

Terry Nance is a graduate of Southwestern Assemblies of God Bible College and Rhema Bible Training Center. He served twenty-three years with Agape Church in Little Rock, Arkansas, as the senior associate and executive director of Agape Missionary Alliance.

Terry is now president of Focus on the Harvest Ministries. His vision is to raise up a new generation of leadership within the local church to stand as armorbearers with their leaders to reach their city, state, nation, and the world with the gospel of Jesus Christ. This ministry is revitalizing the local church through the Armorbearer Leadership School that he conducts weekly in all denominations.

Terry has authored several bestselling books, inspiring thousands of believers to stand with their leaders in faithful service, to help fulfill God's vision, and to submit fully to the Lord.